STATESMEN AND SOLDIERS OF THE CIVIL WAR

Statesmen and Soldiers of the Civil War

Sir Frederick Maurice
George Bagby

Tall Men Books

Contents

LINCOLN AND McCLELLAN AT THE HEADQUARTERS
OF THE ARMY OF THE POTOMAC, OCTOBER, 1862

ISBN: 9798869398017

E-Book ISBN: 9798869398024

This edition was formatted and prepared for
Tall Men Books by George Bagby in 2024.
Cover graphics by Dora.

Foreward

Finding success with his initial American study of *Robert E. Lee: The Soldier (1925)*, Sir Frederick Maurice followed up his work with *Statesmen and Soldiers of the Civil War (1926)*. Maurice chose here to turn his analysis of character and command on the famous executives of the conflict, Davis and Lincoln, and their military captains. Davis' rocky and suspicious relations with Joseph Johnston and his fruitful and trusting relations with Lee both receive treatment. Lincoln's conflicts with McClellan and cooperation with Grant are also analyzed.

Maurice was a man illustrating the practical value of the study of command. *Statesmen and Soldiers* was born, he says, out of conversation on the difficulties of managing the command structure in the first years of the Great War. Lord Kitchener himself, Maurice recalled, referenced the importance of reflection on history to meet the challenges of war. Maurice and Kitchener are sound examples of men with faith in the excellence and competence of the past and of the recently departed norm of belief in heroism. Our own age of deep cynicism still talks about the need to "learn from history" with reference only to the mistakes and evils and the rebels who attacked social order. This study is an example of the constructive approach from an historian of the older school.

George Bagby,
Louisiana, Summer of 2024

Preface

THESE studies of the relations which existed between statesmen and soldiers during the course of a prolonged war were delivered as the Lees-Knowles Lectures for 1925-26 at Trinity College, Cambridge. The idea from which these lectures originated had its germ in a conversation with Lord Kitchener in 1915. Not long after I had joined the headquarters of our Army in France, Lord Kitchener paid his first visit to Sir John French's G.H.Q., then at St. Omer. Early on the morning after Lord Kitchener's arrival I was walking up to the General Staff Office when I saw a tall figure, conspicuous in the blue undress uniform of a field marshal (the rest of us were all in khaki), coming up the hill from Sir John French's house. I stopped and saluted. "Ah,'" said Lord Kitchener, 'I was just coming up to see how you run your office.'"

"Well, sir, we try to make it as little like the War Office as possible.'"

"An admirable ideal; how do you do it?'"

"The practice in the War Office used to be, when a question came up, to collect the largest possible number of opinions about it from everyone who had even the remotest concern with the question, before any attempt was made to arrive at a decision. Here we try to get the question straight to the man who can decide and to get him to do so.'"

"Ah,'" came the answer, "if only we had thought of organizing our Government for war!'"

I knew then nothing of the discussions and controversies which had arisen around the inception of the Dardanelles campaign. But later, when I came in contact with the various attempts made to organize our Government for war, and later still when I read the reports of the Commissions of Enquiry into the Dardanelles and Mesopotamia campaigns, I often recalled Lord Kitchener's words. Before the war I had thought and read about the organization of armies for war, never about the organization of Governments. During the war, when I was asked to think of this, thought was necessarily hurried. Since the war there has been more time for study and reflection and the invitation to give the Lees-Knowles Lectures gave me an occasion for putting the results of reflection into shape.

My historical studies are therefore frankly and unashamedly objective. I had long been dissatisfied that the judgments of Lord Wolseley and of Colonel F. R. Henderson upon Lincoln's conduct of the war, written by the former on incomplete information, and by the latter in a study of one part only of the American Civil War, should stand as the British military criticism of a great statesman. When I studied again, in the light of my own experience in the Great War, the relations between Lincoln and McClellan and between Lincoln and Grant I became more than ever convinced that if, instead of holding up Lincoln's actions in May 1862 as an example of how not to interfere with soldiers, we had made a closer study of the workings of his mind and of the processes by which he evolved a system for the conduct of war, we should have saved ourselves much painful labor in the Great War. That is one reason why I chose the story of the American Civil War as a platform from which to expound my theories; the other I give in the first lecture. The lectures are presented as they were delivered with a few minor alterations and with the addition of the notes and references and some rearrangement of the last two.

November, 1925

F. Maurice

1

Jefferson Davis and J. E. Johnston

It is a commonplace of military textbooks that policy and strategy should go hand in hand. This, like most other attempts to present truth in the form of a caption, is only partially successful. Indeed, without explanation it is misleading, for the picture it is apt to call up of two associates advancing together in close union to their task is not a fair representation of relations which are in reality far more complex than are those of simple comradeship. If analogy be needed I prefer that of parent and child. It is the duty of policy to choose the road for strategy, to set it on its way, to provide means sufficient for the journey, to give timely counsel, to watch the youngster's progress carefully, to be prompt to give a hand should he stumble, to be ready to turn him in a new direction should a change of course seem necessary or opportune, but to resist the temptation to interfere save as a measure of real emergency, and then to make interference as little obvious as may be. It is no easy task to be a wise parent, and as strategy is born only in days of stress and strain the task of father policy is one of special difficulty. It is indeed so difficult that statesmen have not infrequently wrung their hands in despair when it has been thrust upon them. In the midst of the Boer War, Lord Salisbury, then Prime Minister, said: 'I do not think that the British Constitution as at present worked is a good fighting machine."[1] More than one British minister used during the Great War very similar words in conversation with me, and I have listened to French ministers bemoaning the difficulties of conducting war in a democracy, while it was not unusual to hear Germany's military strength ascribed as in a measure due to her autocratic system of government.

Certainly democracy had a very terrible price to pay for victory.

If it be true that modern democracy can neither prevent war nor wage it save at undue cost, its incapacity to deal with what is probably the greatest evil to which modern civilization is exposed is a serious count against that form of government. But before we assume that the charge is true democracy should at least be heard, and there is the more reason for this in that the alternative system of government has a record in the conduct of war which is by no means beyond reproach. It has often been said that the autocratic system is superior, at least in time of war, because it admits of a closer alliance between policy and strategy than any other, but Napoleon, who in his own person directed both, failed to hold the balance between the two, and for that reason more than any other brought about his own downfall and all but ruined his country, while in the Great War Germany's failure to coordinate policy and strategy contributed directly to her defeat, and the memoirs of Ludendorff disclose a state of friction between soldiers and statesmen as great as any that existed in the countries of Germany's enemies.[2]

It would appear then to be at least possible that mistakes in the conduct of war are not necessarily the consequence of any particular form of govern-ment, but that they may be due to causes which are remediable, whether the form of government be an autocracy, a constitutional monarchy, or a republic.

We are too near to the events of the
World War to make it possible to examine dis-
passionately the relations which existed between

statesmen and soldiers in the countries concerned, nor have we yet, save as regards such portions of the war as have been the subject of official inquiry, the material needed to enable us even to begin a judicial examination of questions which bristle with controversy. But some sixty years ago there was fought out a bitter and protracted struggle between two democracies, and the documents relating to the conduct of that struggle are unusually complete and accessible. The similarity in their broad lines of the problems of the American Civil War and of the Great War has struck more than one critic. In both one side held relatively to the other a central position, and it happened in each war that that side which was centrally placed was exposed to the rigors of a blockade. In both there were numerous theatres of war, and in both the coordination of effort was difficult, yet urgently needed. Unity of command is a phrase which appears at an early stage of both struggles in the correspondence of soldiers and statesmen. In both warts there were two main fronts, and in both there was a controversy as to which front should be regarded as decisive. Easterners and Westerners fought in council and on paper sixty years ago as

they did ten years ago. It has seemed to me therefore to be worth while to examine critically, in the
light of our own recent experience, the method of
conducting war adopted by North and South in
the years 1861-1865, in the hope that this inquiry
may help us to decide whether the British Constitution, while—to quote Lord Salisbury again —
"unequaled for producing happiness, prosperity,
and liberty in time of peace,"[3] becomes but a feeble
instrument when battle is joined. Such an inquiry
has this of interest, that it brings into contrast
widely different characters, minds, and methods. It
would be hard to find men more diverse as statesmen than Lincoln and Jefferson Davis, as soldiers
than Lee and Grant. In the clash of personalities
we may hope to discern some spark of truth. .

I propose to begin with Jefferson Davis, who
has been as bitterly criticized as has the leader of
any cause which has been defeated. And this is
natural, for while it is the usual lot of statesmen
and soldiers who have led a people to disaster to
share the obloquy and abuse of quondam friends
and foes, in this case the soldier, Robert E. Lee,
had the rare experience of retaining in defeat the
devoted affection of his men, and of gaining the

respect of his former enemies. There remained therefore but one of the chief targets of criticism, which gained in volume by concentration. Much of this had to do with the causes of the conflict.

I shall confine myself to Davis's administration and direction of the war, and certainly there has been no lack of unfavorable comment upon his handling of those tasks. Lord Wolseley, writing in the nineties,[4] without the material before him which is now available, was particularly severe in his criticism of Davis's administrative capacity, to which the Confederate President replied effectively;[5] and Wolseley was by no means alone, for Davis was accused by many of lacking the most elementary foresight in his preparation for the war. But time has cooled passions, and in recent years historians have appreciated his difficulties and taken a more kindly view of his behavior as war minister.[6] There have been many less competent statesmen in time of war than Jefferson Davis. It happened that he was opposed to a giant, and the inevitable comparison has made him appear to be a dwarf, which he was not. In another milieu he would have appeared to be an administrator of more than average competence; where he failed was in the-general direction of military operations, in combining policy and strategy, and he failed there because he had never worked out in his mind a system for the conduct of war.

When Jefferson Davis was chosen to be President of the Southern Confederacy he possessed an unusual equipment for a statesman confronted with problems of war. The son of a small farmer of the South, he obtained through the influence of an elder brother a nomination to West Point, and passed through the Military Academy at a time when two men with whom he was to be closely associated, Robert E. Lee and J. E. Johnston, were there. He entered the United States cavalry in 1828 and was engaged as a young officer in that Black Hawk War, in which his great opponent Abraham Lincoln served as a volunteer captain. But he tired of military service and, his elder brother having made a fortune as a cotton planter in Mississippi, he left the army to become, like his brother, a successful grower of cotton and employer of slaves. Turning his mind to politics, he was elected to Congress in 1845, and was a member of the Federal Legislature when the Mexican War broke out. He then raised and commanded a regiment of

Mississippi Rifles, which he took to the front, and at the battle of Buena Vista he gained with his regiment a somewhat facile success over the Mexicans, which made him one of the heroes of the war. The effect of this upon his political career was immediate, and may be compared with the consequences of Roosevelt's not dissimilar exploits in Cuba. He was made a Senator at once, became one of the protagonists of the Southern cause and eventually the Southern leader in the Senate. When Pierce was elected President in 1853 he chose Davis as his Secretary of War, and for four years the future leader of the Confederacy controlled the War Department of the United States, returning in 1857 to the Senate to resume his advocacy of the Southern cause. Naturally then, when the breach came, the South turned to him and elected him unanimously to be President. In that position he had, out of such resources as the several States could provide, to create a government, an army, and a navy, to provide the Confederacy with a financial system, to organize the supply of munitions and of war material. If the fact that the North was almost equally unready for war assured him of some leisure for these preparations, their magnitude would

have taxed the capacity of the greatest organizer
with unlimited time at his disposal. The South,
in which the chief industries were the growing
of cotton and tobacco, was poor in manufacturing resources; all the powder factories and most
of the coal and iron were in Northern territory,
while the Federal fleet, if small at the outset, was
sufficiently strong to make communication with
Europe precarious even in the early days of the
struggle. Criticism of Davis's war administration
must therefore be tempered with a sense of the
weight of the burden which he had to carry.

The Confederacy on its creation adopted the
Constitution of the United States, with a preamble
affirming the right of secession and with the addition of clauses securing the right of property in
Negro slaves, and making it the duty of Congress
to protect slavery in any territory which might
subsequently be acquired. Therefore both North
and South possessed a Constitution which conferred on the President such powers as permitted
him, if they did not specifically authorize him, to
act as a dictator in time of war. These powers
were freely used both by Jefferson Davis and by
Abraham Lincoln, and on the whole this attempt

to adapt to the needs of modern democracy the custom of the Roman Republic stood the test of a prolonged war amazingly well. The practice of placing supreme authority temporarily in the hands of one man in a time of great emergency, when rapid decisions are frequently needed, has been proved by the experience of the Civil War to have for the purpose of conducting war most of the advantages which have been claimed for a permanent autocratic system of government. It may however be doubted whether the provision of the Constitution of the United States which makes the President Commander-in-Chief of the Army and Navy proved to be equally wise. The control of military forces by the civil power could be assured in other ways, and the distinction between control and command should be clear. In fact, as we shall see, on such occasions as either President was tempted to exercise the military functions of Commander-in-Chief he was usually unsuccessful, and in the event Jefferson Davis was forced by the pressure of circumstances and of public opinion to hand over those functions to another, while Abraham Lincoln abrogated them voluntarily.

Undoubtedly Jefferson Davis found his military

experience to be of great value when he was shaping his administration; later he was tempted to rely unduly on that experience, and to take too much upon himself — a not uncommon failing with ministers who have some expert knowledge of the department over which they preside. The, greatest asset which he possessed was his knowledge of the character and qualifications of the officers in the army of the United States. His first selections for command from among those who threw in their lot with the South proved him to be an exceptional judge of men. When he moved the Government of the Confederacy from Montgomery to Richmond he found in the capital of Virginia Robert E. Lee, whom he made his military adviser. He sent A. S. Johnston to the Mississippi front, and chose J. E. Johnston and Beauregard to watch the Potomac. It is indeed rare that the selection of four commanders, made before they had undergone the test of battle, proves to have been more than justified at the end of a long war, though it must be confessed that some of Davis's later appointments to command in the West were less happy.

Davis has been accused of lack of energy in providing arms and equipment for the Confederate armies. The best answer to that charge is the fact that the Federal Government, with an established organization, considerable manufacturing facilities, and free access to Europe, made at first little better progress, while our own recent experience of the time it takes to organize the manufacture of munitions and to obtain them from other countries should make us skeptical of suggestions that in the first months of the war Davis should have succeeded in providing arms for all who were willing to fight.[7] He has also been charged with neglecting to use the cotton of the South to provide his administration with financial facilities in Europe. There has been more misunderstanding about the influence of cotton upon the war than about any other of its features. By the time the Confederate Government had been constituted, the whole of the 1860-1861 cotton crop had been exported,[8] and before the '61-'62 crop was ready the Northern blockade had become sufficiently effective to make exportation in bulk impossible. There was no substantial neglect of opportunity. Davis, like most Southerners, had an excessive belief in the influence of "King Cotton" in Europe. His conviction that a cotton famine would certainly cause Great Britain and probably France to intervene undoubtedly influenced his conduct of the war, and here he was wrong in his estimate of the situation. Professor Channing in the latest volume of his *History of the United States*[9] has shown conclusively that when the war broke out there was a glut of cotton in Europe, and that the brokers of Manchester were actually reexporting cotton to Northern ports as late as May 1862. (Before the cotton famine had become severe Lincoln's first Emancipation Proclamation of September 1862, by making abolition the prime issue in the struggle, so enthused popular opinion in Great Britain as to remove what little prospect of British intervention had ever existed, and later the distressed cotton-hands of Lancashire were among those who sent addresses of sympathy and encouragement to the Federal President.[10]

But if Davis was wrong in this respect his administrative measures at the beginning of the war compare favorably with those taken during the same period at Washington. He cannot fairly be accused of lack of foresight, seeing that, when most of his countrymen believed that they would be allowed to secede without fighting, he insisted that the North would fight and fight hard. He was one of the few who foresaw and said publicly that the war would be a long one. He succeeded in getting Congress to change its proposal that first enlistments should be for sixty days, in favor of a term of twelve months. Later he obtained authority for the acceptance of volunteers without limit of numbers for the duration of the war, and in April 1862 he had a Conscription Act passed. In many of these measures he had the advantage of the advice of Lee, but he had the merit both of recognizing good advice when he received it and of acting upon it. The terms of service of the Confederate armies were more judiciously arranged than those of the North, and this fact materially increased the power of resistance of the South.[11]

I have been at pains to answer some of the critics of Davis's war administration and to show my agreement with those who take a kindly view of his capacity, because if he had been merely a blunderer there is clearly nothing to be learned from his experience. Davis was not a great man, but I believe him to have been above the average of war ministers, and during the first year of the war his experience of affairs in general, and of military affairs in particular, made him a formidable opponent of Lincoln, who had had no such experience. His weaknesses were due to his failure to insist that the interests of the Confederacy as a whole should take precedence of the interests of the individual States, to an excess of caution, and to a tendency to rely too much on his small military experience, which caused him to concern himself with minor details. The first of these weaknesses was inherent in the Southern claim to the precedence of the rights of the States, but Davis appears often to have made little effort to get the States to relinquish their several rights for the common good, and even to have gone further sometimes than the States themselves required. One example will suffice. The Confederate law authorized the President to accept-contingents from the States, but left him free to-choose all the commanders of larger formations than regiments. Esprit de corps would naturally be promoted by keeping troops from the same State together under a commander from that State;-but the first essential was that the commander should be efficient. We find Davis writing om October 10, 1861 to Major General G. W. Smith: 'Kentucky has a brigadier but not a brigade; she has however a regiment; that regiment and brigadier might be associated together. Louisiana had regiments enough to form a brigade, but no brigadier in either corps; all of the regiments were sent to that corps which was commanded by a Louisiana general. Georgia has regiments now organized into two brigades; she has on duty with the army two brigadiers, but one of them serves with other troops. Mississippi troops were scattered as if the State were unknown."[12]

There is in this letter, and in a number of others of similar tenor, no hint that military exigencies should be considered, or that commanders should possess some other qualification than a birthplace in a particular State. Ample evidence exists that Davis was subject to considerable political pressure on these and similar matters, but his position was sufficiently strong, at least in the first years of the war, to have made it possible for him to explain to his complainants that military requirements must have precedence over sentimental considerations, and that such matters must be in the hands of the soldiers. As it was, his time was taken up with these details, which he should have insisted on leaving to his war department, and his generals were worried and sometimes even seriously hampered by untimely requests to change commanders and reorganize troops. Later in the war a number of those generals who had most distinguished themselves proved to be Virginians, and in this the influence of Lee, a Virginian, was seen by jealous citizens of other States. There is good reason to believe that the difficulties between Lee and Longstreet, which had very serious consequences for the South, were not remedied by Davis because Longstreet, a gallant man and a good tactician but a bad subordinate, was a favorite son of Georgia, and the President was fearful of offending that State.

This kind of difficulty usually arises when forces have to be raised at the outbreak of war. Kitchener has been considerably criticized because he did not use the existing Territorial Force for the expansion of the British Army in the Great War, but preferred to raise new armies *ab ovo*. The chief factor which influenced him was his memory of the pressure brought by county magnates and persons of influence during the South African War to get units employed at the front which they had raised, or were prepared to raise, according to their fancy, and he feared that similar influences would prevent the development of the systematic organization which he knew to be necessary.[13] The best way to deal with this matter in a country which has not a system of compulsory service, and in which the general public is therefore usually ignorant of the principles and requirements of military organization, is to explain it frankly. A public eager to win the war and not lacking in common sense may be trusted to respond when it knows what is wanted and why it is wanted. If Davis had exercised in this matter the same courage which he displayed in getting adopted the Conscription Act, which might fairly have been considered a violation of State rights, he would have rendered the South a very real service, and incidentally relieved himself of much vexatious labor.

But the Confederate President's desire to foster State sentiment, doubtless for what he believed to be good military reasons, led him to make an even more serious mistake. He organized the

Confederacy into military departments, placing a general in command of all troops in each department. . Such an arrangement, excellent in time of peace, was fatal in time of war, for the military situation took no account of geographical boundaries, while the departments followed in the main State lines. The Mississippi early in the war was seen by the Federals, with their command of the sea, to be a promising line of attack, but the great river was a dividing line between Confederate military departments, and lack of cooperation between them was one of the reasons why Lincoln was able in July 1863 to proclaim that "the Father of Waters goes again unvexed to the sea." Nor was this all; for a great part of the war the only coordinating authority between the several departments was the President himself, and he had neither the military competence nor the leisure to arrange and direct timely concentration. The consequence of this was that the Confederacy failed to obtain the fullest advantage from its central position, which was the greatest strategical advantage it possessed. When Lee was at Davis's side there was combination, and the first battle of Bull Run was won because of J. E. Johnston's opportune junction with

Beauregard. But for a great part of the war Lee was not in Richmond, and combination between departments was then the exception.

It is, however, only fair to Davis to say that in 1861 no power in Europe save Prussia had devised an effective system for the provision of military advice to the head of the State in time of war. Davis's military knowledge was sufficient to keep him from interfering save exceptionally with the operations of his generals in the field, his interference being usually confined to matters of organization and personnel, but that military knowledge was insufficient to enable him to appreciate the difficulties of and the need for unity of direction of forces scattered over a wide area. Failing to understand the difficulties, he could produce no solution. Here is one more example of the danger of a little knowledge. Davis's small experience of war had taught him what a name and an association may mean to soldiers. He recalled the pride which his Mississippi Rifles in the Mexican campaign had taken in their name and in their State connection, and remembered what this had meant in military efficiency. But he did not realize that the command of a battalion in the field might be an inadequate schooling for the direction of a great war.

When the news reached Richmond that the first battle of the war was about to be joined, the soldier in Davis took control. Having once smelled powder, he could not keep away from a battlefield, and he took train for Manassas Junction on the way to Bull Run. The rear even of a victorious army in battle is never a pleasant sight, and the President, on arriving at the junction, met, first stragglers with tales of disaster, then, riding forward to the battlefield, more stragglers and wounded with stories of loss and suffering. He endeavored by personal exhortation to stop what he conceived to be a rout, and was appealing in impassioned tones to the soldiers to rally and to do their duty, when a senior officer, who was having a slight wound dressed near by, told him gruffly that the men were his and had won the day. The officer was Jackson, who had just gained that sobriquet, "Stonewall," with which he was to go down to history.[14]

Having chosen to appear on the battlefield, Davis had to take the consequences. There was no Confederate pursuit after the first battle of Bull

Run, and a disappointed public jumped to the conclusion, from the fact of the President's presence in the field, that there had been political interference with the soldiers. There is no reason to doubt the accuracy of the statement of the two very capable Confederate generals on the spot, J. E. Johnston and Beauregard, that the disorder consequent upon engaging very partially trained troops in battle made pursuit impossible. Pursuit after battle is one of the most difficult operations of war, and the number of successful pursuits, even by highly trained armies, is small. It is possible that pursuit in the air may be a normal sequel of future victories, and have results as deadly as those of Allenby's air pursuit in the battles of Megiddo, but as the nervous strain of battle increases, pursuit on land is likely to be less rather than more frequent. An eager public has always expected, and rarely been gratified by, a dramatic pursuit after victory.

Davis, like his public, expected pursuit after Bull Run. He met J. E. Johnston and Beauregard on the night of the battle, inquired whether pursuit had been ordered, and on hearing that no troops had been sent forward, became the Commander-in-Chief. He asked what troops were available and himself dictated what he proudly claimed after the war was an order for pursuit. It turns out to have been nothing but an order for a reconnaissance by two regiments of infantry, some cavalry, and a battery of artillery, which were ordered to "'scour the country and roads" to the front, to collect wounded and all abandoned stores.[15] A very amateur conception of pursuit after a victory.

If it was not possible for the Confederate troops to advance straight from the field of Bull Run across the Potomac and carry the war into Northern territory, it soon became not only possible but urgently necessary to do this. The North was much depressed by the defeat; the general in command in Washington was expecting and apprehensive of attack.[16] The term of service of the militia, which had been enlisted for three months and formed a considerable part of the Federal army, had expired and new levies were required to replace it. The North had its difficulties in creating a supply of arms and munitions, and was at this early stage of the war far less well supplied than was supposed in the South. The loss of a quantity of war material at Bull Run was therefore a serious matter. Indeed, at no period of the war was the North so vulnerable;

but, given time, the loss would be made good; new armies could be created. Clearly then, the policy for the South was to allow the North as little time as possible for recovery. But it was at this period of the war that Davis showed himself to be at his weakest. Lee had been sent off to conduct a difficult campaign in the mountains of Western Virginia, and the President, left to himself, was seen to have no policy save to protect as much of Southern territory as might be and hope for foreign intervention. This was a futile policy: futile politically, because the border States, Kentucky, Missouri, Western Virginia, and Maryland, were wavering; they might be won by enterprise, they would certainly be lost by inaction; futile militarily, because to give an enemy with superior resources time to develop those resources was to make him a present of what he needed most. The soldiers saw all this. J. E. Johnston, Beauregard, and Gustavus Smith were all agreed that, given reinforcements, which they believed to be available, they could and should take the offensive. But August slipped by, and September, and nothing was done. Then, on October 1, Davis came at Johnston's request to the army for a conference with his generals. Johnston said he needed 19,000 men to enable him to invade Maryland. Smith thought 10,000 would suffice. The President answered that he had not a man to give them. More than the number Johnston asked for were guarding the coasts against possible raids by the Federal fleet. That fleet, weak as it then was, saved the North from a great danger.

In Davis's defense it may be said that there were risks in weakening the garrisons on the coast. The South at this time was uncertain and nervous as to the effect of the war upon the large Negro population in its midst. When the white men went off to the war, women and children were left in the midst of Negroes. There were fears that Federal incursions might be the signal for servile risings, and the President was inundated with demands for the protection of exposed points." Davis, who could never make up his mind to take risks for a great end, yielded to these demands and adopted a policy of passive defense, which he mitigated with proposals for enterprises of so minor an order that one is amazed to find the head of a State permitting himself to be concerned with such details. "I hoped,'" he wrote, "that something could be done by detachments from the army to effect objects less difficult than an advance against his [the enemy's] main force, and particularly indicated the lower part of Maryland, where a small force was said to be ravaging the country and oppressing our friends. This I thought might be feasible by establishing a battery near to Acquia Creek, where the channel of the Potomac was said to be so narrow that our guns could prevent the use of the river by the enemy's boats, and by employing a steamboat lying there, troops enough could be sent over some night to defeat that force and return before any large body could be concentrated against them."[17] The President, instead of devising a policy, plans the emplacement of a battery and the employment of a steamboat load of soldiers!

There is possibly another reason for Davis's reluctance to give Johnston the troops he needed. He disliked the soldier. That dislike may have originated at West Point, where Johnston was a model and Davis but an indifferent cadet. Be that as it may, Johnston, who was Quartermaster-General in the United States Army when he resigned from its service, held, not without some reason, that Davis had treated him unfairly in the matter of his seniority in the Confederate army and expressed his opinion plainly. Davis's answer was brief and discourteous.[18] Lee would never have troubled his head about such a matter, but Johnston was a man of different temper, and Davis as head of the State should have been big enough not to quarrel with him as long as he wanted to use him. In the event, the ill feeling then begun grew and the correspondence between the two shows the existence of friction so constant as to have affected seriously the cause both were serving. Neither of the men was blameless, but of the two Davis is the more blameworthy. He should either not have given Johnston the, most important command in the Confederate army or, having placed him in it, should have trusted him. To retain a general in command and bicker with him is not the act of a statesman. Johnston was one of the three ablest soldiers of the South, and Davis's treatment of him is among the less creditable acts of his Presidency. Davis eventually dismissed him in favor of a gallant but incompetent favorite, and Johnston was only in the last stage of the agony of the Confederacy called back to command by Lee, when Davis had handed his _powers as Commander-in-Chief to that great soldier. Since Davis made no

endeavor to stop Lee's invasions of Northern territory in circumstances certainly not more favorable
than those which existed in the autumn of 1861,
it may be that he had not sufficient confidence in
Johnston to charge him with a mission which he
held to be dangerous. There is little prospect of
harmony between policy and strategy when there
is discord between soldier and statesman.

The price of lost opportunities has to be paid
quickly in war, and the lethargy which followed
the battle of Bull Run created the crisis of the
spring of 1862. That battle, which acted as a spur
to the North, sent the South to sleep. In the latter,
strategy without a lead from policy was helpless.
The people, finding their chiefs inactive, naturally assumed that no special effort was needed,
and were the more alarmed when, before winter
had gone, they found themselves menaced on all
sides. In the west, one Ulysses Grant captured in
February 1862 Forts Henry and Donelson, which
guarded the roads into the Confederacy by the val-
leys of the Tennessee and Cumberland rivers, and
thereby secured control of a great part of Tennessee. Federal naval and military expeditions had in
March captured Hatteras Inlet and Roanoke Island

off the coast of North Carolina, and Port Royal on the coast of South Carolina. The blockade was becoming more and more effective, and, greatest danger of all, a large and well-equipped army had been assembled and organized by McClellan on the Potomac, before the menace of which J. E. Johnston had retreated. Alarm in the South was turning to consternation, and the President who had been the hero of 1861 became the target of criticism and abuse. But Davis appeared at his best in an emergency, and in this one he did a brave thing. Robert E. Lee, loudly acclaimed when he placed his sword at the service of his State, had proved a disappointment. The public, unaware of the valuable work he had done quietly in council and in office, knew only that he had been sent to command a force in Western Virginia and had failed. But Davis had learned his value, and now calling him to his side as military adviser, made possible a swift change in the fortunes of war.

Notes:
1. Hansard: House of Lords, January 30, 1900.

2. Ludendorff: *My War Memories, 1914-18*, and
The General Staff and Its Problems.

3. Hansard: House of Lords, January 30, 1900.

4. *North American Review*, vol. CXLIX, p. 1390.

5. *Ibid.*

6. See Ropes: *The Story of the Civil War — to the
Opening of the Campaigns of 1862*, p. 107. Rhodes:
History of the Civil War, p. 33.

7. The statement made by Henderson, *Stonewall
Jackson*, vol. I, p. 264, ""The President, too, while
the markets of Europe were still open, neglected
to buy in a store of munitions of war; it was not
till May that an order was sent across the seas and
then only for 10,000 muskets," and Lord Wolseley's criticism of Davis on the same count appear
to have been based upon a similar statement in
Battles and Leaders of the Civil War. These critics
overlooked Davis's very clear statement in vol. I,
pp. 311 and 471-483 of his *Rise and Fall of the Confederate Government,* which is amplified in his reply
to Wolseley in the *North American Review.* Davis
shows that on February 21, 1861, three days after
his inauguration as President, he sent Captain

Semmes, later the commander of the famous Alabama, to the North, "'to make purchases of arms, ammunition, and machinery.'" Captain Semmes found little difficulty in placing contracts, but the vigilance of the civil authorities prevented export. Early in April Major Huse was sent to England for a like purpose, but, as might be expected, he "found few serviceable arms upon the market." Private manufacturers do not keep stocks of weapons of war. Huse, however, placed contracts, but when these matured the British Government prevented shipment. Huse wrote December 30, 1861, from London: "It is miserable to have to look at the immense pile of packages in the warehouse at St. Andrews wharf and not be able to send anything." Then follows a long list of war material, beginning with 25,000 rifles. It was not quite such a simple matter for the South to obtain munitions in Europe as some of Davis's critics imagined.

8. See Davis: *North American Review,* vol. CKLIX (1890), p. 482.

9. Channing: *History of the United States,* vol. VI, ch. 12.

10. One of those addresses is preserved in Lincoln's tomb at Springfield, Illinois.

11. The Federal militia which fought at the first battle of Bull Run was enlisted for three months and their service expired immediately after the battle was over. Until a late period of the war the Federal commanders were hampered by having to let men go because their engagement was ended.

12. Davis: *Rise and Fall,* vol. 1, p. 4453

13. Arthur: *Life of Lord Kitchener,* vol. Ill, p. 309.

14. Alexander: *The American Civil War,* p. 42.

15. The actual order dictated by Davis was not sent, but another, of which I have given the substance above, was issued by Beauregard. This order Davis says was "to the same effect" as his own. See *Rise and Fall,* p. 352 et seq.

16. See *McClellan's Own Story,* p. 87.

17. Davis: *Rise and Fall,* vol. 1, p. 452.

18. It ran (Hughes: *General Johnston,* p. 86): "Sir, I have received and read your letter of the 12th instant. The language is as you say unusual, its arguments and statements utterly one-sided, and its insinuations as unfounded as they are unbecoming. I am, etc., Jefferson Davis,'"

2

———

Jefferson Davis and Lee

WHEN Lee rejoined Davis at Richmond on March 13, 1862, to be charged "with the conduct, under the President, of all the military operations in the Confederacy,"[1] he found "the enemy pushing us back in all directions."[2] Beauregard had been detached from J. E. Johnston and had gone with reénforcements to the west, but this had not prevented the fall of Forts Henry and Donelson. The number and enterprise of the Federal expeditions against the coast had spread fear along the Atlantic shores of the Confederacy; but none of these dangers caused such alarm and disillusionment as did the retreat of the victorious army of Bull Run when McClellan's preparations for the invasion of Virginia at length matured.

One of Davis's characteristics was a curiously dogged obstinacy, which made him, while loath to encourage or even permit offensive adventures, regard retreat as an indefensible weakness, even when retreat was obviously the correct military course.[3] He complained to Johnston that he had not been told when the army was to fall back, and grumbled because retreat entailed the abandonment at Manassas of some immobile heavy guns which had been sent to Johnston despite his protest, and the loss of a supply depot which had been located without consulting the military commander.' Johnston rightly continued to retreat as McClellan's movement to the Yorktown peninsula developed, and the relations between him and the President grew worse and worse. In April he was sent into the peninsula to delay McClellan, and again he had to fall back. In the last stage of this retreat he crossed the Chickahominy and took position some distance behind that river. The President, riding out to the army, was alarmed to find some of Johnston's field artillery in the very suburbs of Richmond. The lively interview which followed is thus described by Davis: "General Johnston's explanation of this to me unexpected movement was that he thought the water of the Chickahominy unhealthy and had directed the troops to cross and halt at the first good water on the southern side, which he supposed would be found near the river. He also adverted to the advantage of having the river in front rather than in rear of him — an advantage certainly obvious enough, if the line was to be near to it on either of its banks."[4] Davis's slight military knowledge led him to the amateur conception that the right way to defend a river was to line its banks. Johnston's plan was to wait till McClellan was astride the river and then to attack, when, to quote Lincoln's shrewd words to one of his generals[5] who proposed to make such a crossing, "he was entangled upon the river, like an ox jumped half over a fence and liable to be torn by dogs in front and rear, without a fair chance to gore one or kick the other."[6]

Johnston would disclose nothing of his military plans, and the President, racked with anxiety for the safety of the Confederate capital, was angry and perplexed. "'Seeing no preparations," he wrote, 'to keep the enemy at a distance, and kept in ignorance of any plan for such purpose, I sent for General R. E. Lee, then at Richmond in general charge of army operations, and told him why and how I was dissatisfied with the conditions of affairs. He asked me what I thought it was proper to do. Recurring to a conversation held about the time we had together visited General Johnston, I answered that McClellan should be attacked on the other side of the Chickahominy before he had matured his preparations for the siege of Richmond. To this he promptly assented, as I anticipated he would, for I knew it had been his opinion. He then said, "General Johnston should of course advise you of what he expects or proposes to do. Let me go and see him and defer this discussion till I return."'[7] Lee saw Johnston and got him to tell the President enough to relieve the latter's anxiety; McClellan was attacked while he was astride the Chickahominy, as Johnston had intended; and if the battle of Seven Pines was far from being a decisive victory for the Confederacy, it at least gained for Lee an invaluable month in which to mature his plans for the defense of Richmond.

Curiously enough, just at the time when friction between the head of the Confederacy and his chief commander in the field was near to bringing disaster, similar friction between Lincoln and McClellan, due to a like cause, was the main reason why the Union powers were unable to extract any permanent advantage from the very favorable position which they had gained in the spring of 1862. Neither Johnston nor McClellan understood that the head of the State has the right to be assured, when the State is in danger, that everything possible is being done for its protection. The "damned politician" is often a nuisance to the soldier, particularly when he pretends to military knowledge which he does not possess; but the statesman is, even from the purely military point of view, the indispensable ally of the soldier, and should be treated as such.

It is a peculiarly difficult matter for the general in the field to decide just how much of his plans he should make known to his political chief. Napoleon used to say that if he thought his pillow knew his military secrets he would burn it, and the danger of disclosing intentions is obvious. The execution and ultimate success of military plans is usually subject to a score of unforeseen and unforeseeable contingencies, and to appear to promise more than is fulfilled may have the effect of undermining the very confidence which information is intended to create.[8] General Nivelle in 1917 made the mistake of explaining to the Allied statesmen the complete details of a very ambitious scheme which in the event could not be carried through. But it may be taken as a general rule that, if the soldier does not satisfy the statesman as to the protection provided for the vitals of the State, he is likely to suffer far more than he will gain by secrecy. Johnston was clearly wrong in not letting Davis know how he proposed to protect Richmond, and Lee was clearly right in saying that Johnston should of course have advised the President of what he proposed to do.

I have said enough to indicate that Davis was not an easy man to deal with, and he must have been particularly trying to Johnston in those critical days. The President had the habit of riding out from Richmond — sometimes with a considerable cortége[9] — to the army even on days when it was engaged with the enemy. Johnston was wounded in the battle of Seven Pines and his staff believed that he received his injury because he rode out to the extreme front in order to avoid Davis, whom he saw approaching.[10] Davis immediately appointed Lee to the command of the army. During the first of Lee's battles the Confederate President, following his custom, appeared on the field with a more than usually large suite of hangers-on. Lee, turning to him, asked, "'Who are all this army of people, and what are they doing here?'"

"It is not my army, General," answered Davis.

"It is certainly not my army, Mr. President, and this is no place for it," came the reply.

"Well, General," said Davis, "if I withdraw perhaps they will follow." He rode away, and thereafter his visits to the army became less frequent and more private.[11]

Lee's dealings with the President were in very
marked contrast to those which prevailed between
Davis and Johnston. He appreciated to a nicety
the relations which should exist between himself
and the head of the State. He invariably treated
the President with the most complete courtesy

and respect, gave him all necessary information, and being himself completely devoid of personal ambition or of any trace of self-seeking, he never aroused in his chief, who was inclined to be both arrogant and jealous, the faintest suspicion that he coveted powers which should belong to the President. He was often tried by Davis every whit as highly as Johnston had been, but through all these trials he showed a remarkable understanding of Davis's difficulties and problems, and he continued quietly and tactfully to educate him in the principles of strategy and of the conduct of war. In one respect Lee failed. He could not induce Davis until too late to fill the place which he had occupied as military adviser, and his own extreme modesty and reluctance to push himself forward prevented him from asking for increased authority and powers for himself.

The Federal incursion into Tennessee, though checked on April 7, 1862, by the battle of Shiloh, had aroused the Southerners to the fact that they were engaged in a war on two fronts, while the loss of New Orleans on May 1 showed them that their enemy was capable of creating a third. There was, however, no argument at first as to which was to be considered the main front. McClellan by his advance on Richmond settled that, just as Ludendorf in March 1918 settled a similar question in a greater war. We may carry the comparison still further, for McClellan produced unity of command of the Confederate as Ludendorff did of the Allied armies. But in 1862 unity of command did not last long. Begun on March 13, 1861, it ended on the following June 1, when Lee took command of the Army of Northern Virginia. Within that short period much was accomplished. It saw the passing of the Conscription Act, to which I have already referred; ' a noteworthy increase in the Confederate forces; the transfer, to what was by general consent the vital theatre of war, of forces which the President had heretofore believed to be indispensable in their locations; and within that theatre of war those remarkable combinations, planned by Lee's genius and brilliantly executed by Stonewall Jackson, which led to the relief of Richmond from imminent danger. It may be said in Davis's defense that the Confederacy did not possess two Lees, and that he was put to it to find capable soldiers to command in all the fields in which the Confederacy was threatened. But it is impossible to avoid the suspicion that it was as much his dislike of Johnston as the urgency of the crisis which had caused him to bring Lee to Richmond, and when the crisis was passed, when Lee had driven McClellan to the bank of the James and was driving Pope backwards to the Potomac, he felt himself to be fully competent to direct once more the armies of the Confederacy. Had he possessed his great opponent's power of learning from experience, he would in July 1862 have done what Abraham Lincoln did in March 1864, and placed the man who had proved himself to be conspicuously his ablest soldier in general control of all his armies.

When Lee had driven Pope's army in confusion from the field of the second battle of Bull Run, he succeeded in avoiding the hesitations and delays which followed the first Confederate victory near that stream. Davis's military policy had been, as I have said, to defend Southern territory and hope for foreign intervention. Lee had induced him to modify this, and the President, with a characteristic touch of military pedantry, now favored a strategy to which he gave the high-sounding title of "'offensive-defensive." The soldier attached no importance to labels. His first object had been to drive the Federals out of Virginia, and his second was to keep them out of his native State. He wanted-to retain the initiative. Therefore while Pope's men were seeking safety behind the Potomac he set his troops in motion to cross that river into Maryland, and, satisfied that he had given the President some notion of the value of offense, told him that he had done so. 'We cannot afford to be idle," he wrote, "and though weaker than our opponents in men and military equipment, must endeavor to harass if we cannot destroy them."[12]

But Lee's statement in the same letter that his "army was not properly equipped for an invasion of an enemy's territory," with its clear intimation that now was the time to strengthen him with re-inforcements, could not move Davis. "The fact is that, despite all the President's admiration for and confidence in Lee, the policies of the two men were never really in agreement. Davis could not bring himself to withstand the incessant appeals to him for protection, which came to him from all parts of the Confederacy, or to overcome the reluctance of the several States to denude them-selves of troops, mainly because he was not so constituted as to be able to take great risks for great ends' Lee's policy was clear from the first. He saw that the South must seize every opportunity with both hands, and endeavor to enforce a satisfactory peace before the North had time to develop its resources. On the eve of the war he had written: "An union that can only be maintained by swords and bayonets . . . has no charms for me";[13] and he believed, not without reason, that there were many in the North who shared that view. He held, therefore, that the best way to make that the opinion of the majority was to display a victorious Confederate army in Northern territory, and he was prepared to dare much to bring this about. In Davis's mind the risks always loomed greater than the promise of success, and so not even in the high tide of Lee's success was there any real union of Confederate policy and strategy, the chief reason for this being that there was no one in Richmond to view and advise the President on the military problem as a whole. Lee's army, weak in numbers and poor in equipment, was forced by McClellan back into Virginia, and the opportunity of enforcing peace, which he had sought, disappeared.[14]

In the autumn of 1862 McClellan's dilatoriness

finally wore out Lincoln's patience, and he was removed to give place to Burnside, who advanced towards Fredericksburg on the Rappahannock, the shortest land route from Washington to Richmond. Lee was disposed to meet the movement by allowing Burnside to advance so that he might have room to maneuver against the Federal flanks and communications. It was the wiser course, for a general who had confidence in his own powers and in the mobility of his troops, to endeavor to create opportunities for striking his opponent at a disadvantage, than to plant himself athwart the enemy's line of advance, in the hope that the enemy would be unwise enough to come and knock his head against a position selected and occupied for defense. This plan Lee explained in outline to the President at Richmond on November 20,[15] that is, three days after Burnside had assumed command. But Davis's old dislike of yielding territory to the foe returned as soon as there were indications that Burnside was marching on Fredericksburg. He wanted him to be opposed on the Rappahannock. Lee did not wish to do this, for the good and sufficient reason that the heights on the left or Federal bank of the river dominated those on the right or

Confederate bank, and knowing the ground well, he perceived that, while it might not be a hard task to repulse a direct attack, it would be very difficult if not impossible to follow up that attack across the river, while the enemy held the hills which commanded the crossings. He wanted not to repulse an attack but to win such a victory as would have great consequences. In the event, the weather became wet and stormy in November and the roads were deep in mud. The knowledge that he might not, in these circumstances, be able to maneuver quickly probably decided Lee to fall in with the President's views without further protest and to meet Burnside at Fredericksburg, where the inept Federal attack was easily repulsed; but there was no pursuit. The Confederate press was vocal in criticism of the failure to follow up the victory, and more mature comment of the same tenor has not been lacking. The best reply is that both Lee and Jackson[16] had foreseen before the battle that the criticism would arise.

I have cited the incident, as it is an example of the kind of interference with a general in the field which is never justifiable, though in this instance the interference probably — as I have pointed out —had no effect upon Lee's plans. Neither Fredericksburg nor the Rappahannock River had any political significance in November 1862, and there was no justification for Davis's proposition to Lee that the Confederate army should oppose Burnside there. The most that any statesman in Richmond — or indeed any soldier there, if one had the authority — should have said to Lee was, "It is important that Burnside's invasion of Virginia should be checked as soon as possible'; and Lee should have been left to find the way to defeat the enemy. The situation might have been entirely different if some special importance attached to the possession of Fredericksburg, or if the town had been the gauge of prolonged battle, such as Ypres or Verdun became in the Great War. The statesman in such a case would have been justified in saying to his general, ""Hold this place to the last. The morale of the people at home is shaky and will not stand its loss'; or, "I am engaged in some highly critical negotiations with foreign Powers. The loss of this famous place would have a very serious effect at this time. Therefore hold on to it like grim death.""

"There may be, indeed there often are, political

considerations which must influence and in extreme cases may dictate military actions, even in such matters as how, when, and where to accept or to refuse battle; but the wise statesman will weigh those considerations very carefully before he passes them on with any suggestions for action to the commander in the field. The man in the office chair should remember always that advice and plans framed at a distance are usually either mischievous or inapplicable when they reach the front.

The winter which followed the battle of Fredericksburg was necessarily a period of inaction. For the soldiers of the Army of Northern Virginia it was a bitter season, and one can but wonder, when one recalls the rations which modern armies receive, how Lee's men kept their health on a daily quarter of a pound of meat. There was no serious deficiency of supplies in the Confederacy, but it was a difficult matter with bad roads, and with the most serviceable horses in the armies, to collect them from the farmers, and a still more difficult matter to distribute them, when collected, to the troops. The Southern railways in the sixties were neither numerous nor well equipped. Many of the railway personnel had been Northerners and were not easily replaced; most of the repairing shops were in the North, and thence had come most of the replacements required. Considering all the difficulties, it is not fair to charge Davis's administration with neglect of the provision of supplies, but these difficulties had consequences which with a better understanding of the principles of the conduct of war could have been avoided.

"In order to relieve the strain on the railway which sent him the food for his army, Lee agreed to a proposal from Richmond that Longstreet with two of his divisions should go into the district south of the James.[17] Lee bargained that Longstreet should be ready to return to him promptly, but, with the consent of the authorities in Richmond, that General became involved in a wholly useless siege of Suffolk, which was garrisoned by a Federal force approximately equal to his own. When April came and Hooker, who had taken Burnside's place, began to show signs of activity,

Lee's thoughts turned to Longstreet's divisions. But Longstreet was involved in his siege, and his wagons were away collecting supplies, so when the summons came he could not move quickly, and he did not rejoin Lee until the battle of Chancellorsville was ended. Had his 20,000 been present, it is reasonable to suppose that the result of that battle would have been more conclusive than it actually was.

Here then was a military situation with which neither the President, burdened with many cares, nor the civilian Secretary of War, who was little more than the registrar of Davis's decisions, could cope. It required a competent soldier at headquarters, capable of watching and gauging the situation both on Lee's and on Longstreet's front, capable also of estimating accurately the time required for a military movement. With such a man, a timely concentration would have been possible; without him, it was not. Davis evidently felt this to be so. He was sufficient of a soldier to realize that there was something radically wrong with arrangements which brought Longstreet to a battlefield just after the last shot was fired. He began to long for competent advice, but he had not the knowledge — which, as I have explained, was very far from being general in the sixties — to enable him to see what was defective in his organization, or how to remedy the defect.

In the spring of 1863 the problem of the two fronts clamored for decision. Grant's campaign against Vicksburg was fully developed, and was making alarming progress. There could be no question as to the importance of the Mississippi to the Confederacy. If the South lost control of the great river it would be severed. Louisiana, Arkansas, and Texas, States from which came many of the best soldiers and much of the sorely needed supplies, would be cut off from the remainder. Was a supreme effort to be made to prevent such a disaster? The answer to that question involved a wider one. What was the war policy of the Confederacy? How did it hope to wring from the North a satisfactory peace? Was the right policy to trust to wearing out the patience and endurance of the North, and to foreign intervention? In that event the main efforts of the Confederacy should have been devoted to saving Vicksburg and the Mississippi. It was not to be expected that the repulse of Grant would be regarded in the North as such a calamity as would bring nearer a peace satisfactory to the South, but it would remove a pressing danger and might make a prolonged resistance more possible.

Alternatively, was the war policy to be to follow up the victory of Chancellorsville, which, coming so soon after Burnside's disastrous assault at Fredericksburg, had greatly depressed the North, by making a final effort to confront the Federals With a victorious Confederate army in their territory, as a prelude to proposing terms of peace? If that were to be the policy, then there was no time to lose in giving it effect. The man power of the Confederacy, which Davis's administrative measures had developed more quickly than had the Northern statesmen their supply of men, was beginning to show the strain of a prolonged war. The South could not hope to be able in the future to place larger armies in the field. The blockade was becoming daily more severe, and the provision of munitions more difficult, while the resources of the North were even yet not fully developed. Then again, if the defeat of Grant was to become the prime military object of the Confederacy, the army in Virginia would be perforce inactive; the Federal Army of the Potomac would recover from the effect of Chancellorsville and would not be idle. Suppose the Army of the Potomac were to begin another advance on Richmond while the main forces of the Confederacy were engaged with Grant; would Richmond be secure? Was it more important to preserve Vicksburg than to save Richmond from danger?

These were terrible questions for a harassed statesman. Davis, with no responsible military adviser at his side to review them for him and propound a solution, and with no organized system for the conduct of war, was torn by conflicting advice. He had done what seemed to him best. When J. E. Johnston had recovered from his wound, he, to his honor, overcame his dislike of the soldier, and sent him to command in the west. Therefore when the crisis came he had his two ablest soldiers in military control in the two main theatres of war. He made no attempt to interfere with their military plans, but supported them as he considered he best could, while urgent calls for help were pouring in to him from many quarters. He did not know how to do more for them, and failed to give them what they wanted most —a clear-cut policy.

As often happens in such crises, there were too many military cooks preparing the broth. Longstreet, passing through Richmond on his way to rejoin Lee, proposed a concentration for the relief of Vicksburg. It was not very cordially received, and he remarks: "Foreign intervention was the ruling idea with the President, and he preferred that as the easiest solution of all problems."[18] Davis had throughout the war an undue faith in foreign intervention, but I doubt if that faith influenced his decision at this time. Beauregard had a very similar plan to Longstreet's and he elaborated it at some length.[19]

Now the one soldier upon whom Davis had learned to lean was Lee, and Lee had a remarkable faculty for sticking to his own job and not interfering with those of other people. He had, as I have said, a great respect for the President as the head of the State, and understood the complexities of Davis's position probably better than any other of the Confederate generals. He had also a very keen sense of the soldier's position as the servant of the civil power, but he probably failed to understand how little the President was able to view the situation clearly as a whole and how anxious Davis was to be advised wisely. Lee's function was to propose a plan of campaign for his army which the President could accept or reject. Fully engrossed with the cares of that army, he did not feel himself to be in a position to decide on the military policy of the Confederacy, and he made no attempt to step outside what he held to be his function in order to thrust advice upon the President.

Davis was eager to give Lee greater powers, but did not know how to set about it. He proposed in June 1863 to place him in command of all troops, not only in Virginia but also in the Carolinas, while leaving him in executive command of the Army of Northern Virginia. Lee at once telegraphed to the President: "'I cannot operate in this manner. I request you to give such orders as your judgment dictates."[20] He was right to refuse, while in direct command of one body of troops, to attempt to issue orders to other bodies at a distance. Davis's ignorance that this was not good military organization may be excused when we remember that both the Germans and the Allies not only proposed but actually made a similar mistake in the Great War.[21] Where Lee was wrong was in not realizing that the President earnestly desired to help him, and in not telling him how to do it. But this meant that Lee should propose to be relieved of the immediate command of the Army of

Northern Virginia, to which he was bound by close ties of affection and comradeship, and be given the authority and means to direct all the forces of the Confederacy. It was not in the man's character that he should so suggest his own advancement.

Lee had a definite war policy. Davis had none. The soldier held that the one way in which the South could end the war to its satisfaction was to establish an army firmly in Northern territory. He had repeatedly told the President that the Army of Northern Virginia should take the offensive at the first possible. moment; and now, after listening to Longstreet's proposal for a campaign against Grant, he did not change his mind, but planned to follow the victory of Chancellorsville with an invasion of Pennsylvania. Having a skilled soldier's knowledge of the changes and chances of war and a reluctance to appear to promise too much, he did not make it sufficiently clear to the President that the time had come to stake everything on the result of an offensive campaign. With ample experience of the sensitiveness of the authorities in Washington to a threat on the Federal capital, he hoped that his movement would at least prevent the dispatch of reinforcements to Grant, and might even cause the withdrawal of Federal troops from the Mississippi. But the relief of Vicksburg was in his mind a secondary matter. His real purpose was to end the war, and as he wrote to Davis on June 10, 1863, "to neglect no honorable means of weakening and dividing our enemies. We should give all the encouragement we can consistently with truth to the rising peace party in the North."[22]

While it is perhaps fair to say that Lee should have been more bluntly explicit, and have understood that the administration at Richmond, being improvised, was without either the practice or the tried machinery of an established government, yet, reading the correspondence of the two men, it is not possible to acquit Davis of the charge of obtuseness and lack of enterprise. The President's confidence in Lee made him approve the plan for the invasion of Pennsylvania, but he never seems to have grasped that this was the Confederacy's last throw for victory, and he did not give Lee the support which the Army of Northern Virginia might have received if there had been a man at Richmond who was prepared to take risks elsewhere in order that by invasion peace might be won. In the situation in which the Confederacy found itself at the beginning of the summer of 1863, it was not worth attempting to cross the Potomac unless the attempt were made with every man, gun, and horse the Confederacy could by hook or by crook send to the Army of Northern Virginia. Davis describes the reasons which made him approve Lee's plans as follows: "It was decided by a bold movement to attempt to transfer hostilities to the north side of the Potomac, by crossing the river and marching into Maryland and Pennsylvania, simultaneously driving the foe out of the Shenandoah Valley. Thus it was hoped that General Hooker's army would be called from Virginia to meet our advance towards the heart of the enemy's country. In the event, the vast preparations which had been made for an advance on Richmond would be foiled, the plan of his summer campaign deranged, and much of the season for active operations be consumed in the new combinations and dispositions that would be required. If beyond the Potomac some opportunity should be offered so as to enable us to defeat the army on which our foe most relied, the measure of our success would be full, but if the movement only resulted in freeing Virginia from the presence of the hostile army it was more than could fairly be expected from awaiting the attack which was clearly indicated."[23]

Davis, like Napoleon's opponents, saw too many things at once. He failed to grasp his General's main purpose, and allowed his mind to be diverted by the subsidiary advantages of the plan which had been put to him. If he, like the Emperor, had seen but one thing at a time, the defeat of the Federal army beyond the Potomac, and had given his whole mind to strengthening Lee for that end, the campaign of Gettysburg might have had a different issue. As it was, though defeated, Lee did by his invasion foil until the following spring "'the vast preparations for an advance upon Richmond'"; but with the loss of Gettysburg and Vicksburg the last chance of a Southern triumph had gone. Torn between two fronts, Davis lost on both.

We need not for my purpose follow the Confederacy to its downfall. By brilliant generalship Lee delayed the issue, and after the fateful struggle of Gettysburg the war dragged on through the autumn and winter of 1863, throughout the whole of '64, and on into the spring of '65. But delay was

— as Lee had foreseen it would be — fatal to the South, and never again after the summer of 1863 were there opportunities which a skillful combination of statecraft and strategy could use to save the Confederacy from its fate. The greatest soldier of modern times could not do more than win victories in the field. He needed, in the circumstances of the time, the aid of a great statesman to make victory decisive, and the great statesman was in Washington, not in Richmond.

But, it may reasonably be asked, if a great statesman is the necessary complement of a great soldier, how can any nation reasonably expect to have both when a crisis comes? The answer is that we to-day are not living in the circumstances of 1863. We have had, and may learn from, experiences which Davis had not. A reasonable competence in statesmen and soldiers is not sufficient to prevent disaster. As Lord Salisbury pointed out in the speech I have already quoted, every war of any importance in which Great Britain was engaged in the nineteenth century began unfortunately. "We cannot," said he, "have been so unfortunate as to have fought four times and to have lighted upon the most incompetent and worthless ministers the world has ever seen." In each of those four wars to which Lord Salisbury referred, the Walcheren Expedition, the Peninsular War, the Crimean War, and the South African War, our troubles, like those of Davis, arose far more because we had evolved no system for the conduct of war than because of any exceptional lack of capacity in our statesmen. It requires an Abraham Lincoln to devise in the stress of war a sound system for its conduct when none has been prepared beforehand. But a Davis is well capable of administering the affairs of a nation at war when that nation has considered in time the respective functions of statesman and soldier.

Notes:

1. *Official Records*, vol. IV, p. 223.

2. Letter to Mrs. Lee, March 14, 1862.

3. He said in October 64, "Does anyone imagine that we can conquer the Yankees by retreating before them?" And three months before he made that characteristic statement he removed J. E. Johnston from his command in the west because that general was retreating before Sherman.

His aversion to retreat revived all his prejudices against Johnston, who at the time when he was discharged was carrying through a series of prudent and well-planned delaying operations.

4. Davis: *Rise and Fall*, vol. Vl, p. 103.

5. Hooker.

6. *O. R.*, vol. XXVII, part 1, p. 31.

7. Davis: *Rise and Fall*, vol. Il, p. 120.

8. An example of Lee's tact and knowledge of how to handle the President was given at a war council held in Richmond in the middle of April 1862, to decide whether Johnston should go down to Yorktown to oppose McClellan or await him outside Richmond as he wanted to do. Lee wanted Johnston to go to Yorktown in order to gain time for his combinations with Jackson, which he was already planning. The issue of those combinations was doubtful and their success depended upon secrecy. Lee said not a word about them at the council, but knowing the President's reluctance to give up Southern territory, he gained his support for sending Johnston into the peninsula on other grounds.

9. Editor's Footnote: an official entourage

10. Alexander: *The American Civil War*, p. 92.

11. Eckenrode: *Jefferson Davis*, p. 180.

12. *O. R.*, vol. XIX, p. 590.

13. Letter to his son, January 23, 1861.

14. After entering Maryland, Lee wrote to Davis, September 8, 1862, suggesting that the time had come to propose peace to the North. *O. R.*, vol. XIX, part U, p. 60.

15. *Lee's Confidential Dispatches to Davis*, p. 66, and O. R., vol. XXI, p- 1021.

16. Dabney: *Life and Campaigns of Thomas J. (Stonewall) Jackson*, p. 595.

17. The Confederate Commissary-General in Richmond had said: "'If the army wants more food, let it use fewer passenger coaches.'"

18.Longstreet: *From Manassas to Appomattox*, p. 327

19. *0. R.*, vol. XXXV, p. 836.

20. *Lee's Confidential Dispatches to Davis*, p. 99.

21. In August 1914 von Moltke during the first German invasion in the west placed their First Army under the command of von Bulow, who was retained in command of the Second Army. The result was confusion and failure to

seize opportunity, In March 1917 the Allies placed the British Army under the direction of General Nivelle, who was kept in executive command of the French armies. The result was that Nivelle, occupied with the business of his own command, failed to appreciate the significance of the German retreat to the Hindenburg line, which began on the British front, and this failure had a disastrous effect on his whole campaign.

22.*O.R.*, vol. XXVII, part m1, pp. 881 et seq.

23. Davis: *Rise and Fall,* vol. Il, p. 437.

3

Abraham Lincoln and McClellan

WAR found the North with a President who, with little administrative and less military experience, was far from being master in his own house. As a Republican, Lincoln had a majority neither in the House nor in the Senate, and there were members of his own Cabinet who regarded his homely manner with amused contempt. On the one hand, he was accused by some of his most ardent supporters of weakness in not at once proceeding to extreme measures against the South; on the other hand, many of his political opponents, and probably up to April 12, 1861, a majority of the people of the North, regarded the idea of civil war as too horrible to contemplate. Now the first task of a statesman confronted with the issue of peace or war is, if war cannot be avoided, to bring his people united into the struggle. That unity is in the narrower military sphere of such importance as in many cases to override the gain of prompt action.

Certainly the Power which, on entering war, strikes first and strikes quickly obtains great military advantages, but if those advantages are purchased at the price of political dissension at home they may, they probably will, be found to have cost too much.

There were many among us who in August 1914 held that in delaying to mobilize until three days after the French we had seriously prejudiced our chances in the war. I am unable to see that, if the British Expeditionary Force had appeared at Mons three days earlier than it did, the military situation would have been materially altered in our favor, ot that those French critics who are wont to ascribe the loss of the battles on the Belgian frontier to our tardy appearance in France

have made good their case. It is indeed not impossible that, if an earlier arrival had caused us to
advance farther into Belgium, it might have made
our situation more perilous than it in fact was. In
any event, we could not by a more prompt mobilization have secured any advantage comparable
to that of the unity at home, which the violation
of Belgium's neutrality evoked.[1] There are other
things to be considered in deciding when and how
to proceed to war than the importance of obtain-
ing the initiative.

On March 4, 1861, in his first Inaugural, Lincoln
had thus addressed the South: "In your hands, my
dissatisfied fellow countrymen, and not in mine is
the momentous issue of civil war. The Government will not assail you. You can have no conflict
without being yourselves the aggressors." That
policy was from the military standpoint the best
possible for the North. I am not going to discuss
the rights and wrongs of the bombardment of Fort
Sumter, over which much ink has been spilled.
The outstanding fact is that the measures which
Lincoln carried through in face of the opposition
of his own Cabinet resulted in the Confederacy
firing, on April 11, the first shot at the Union flag;

and that shot did more towards increasing the military strength of the North than any action by its Government could have achieved. As Artemus Ward puts it in his quaint account of his interview with Jefferson Davis: "But, J. Davis, the minit you fire a gun at the piece of dry goods called the Star-Spangled Banner the North gets up and rises en massy, in defense of that banner." As we shall see, the North had some difficulty in rising "en massy," but it entered upon the war with an enthusiasm greater than the most optimistic had believed possible a month before, and for this the credit is due to Lincoln's statecraft.

Next to creating unity among his people, the most important business of a statesman in war is to detach support from his enemy, and to add it to his own country. The attitude of the States bordering the Confederacy was at the outset of the war more than doubtful. In Kentucky and Missouri the State authorities were definitely Southern in their sympathies, and the majority of the legislature of Maryland held the same views. The mountain folk of Western Virginia were for the Union, but could they be detached from the bulk of the State? By prompt action Western Virginia was detached and eventually made a separate State, and the others, though in the case of Missouri only after a considerable struggle, were preserved to the Union. Many men from all these States joined the Confederate ranks, but more supported the Union in arms, and the State governments remained under Union control. Therefore Lincoln, despite his administrative inexperience, was able from the first to do, in those matters most important for military success, that which might have baffled the skill of a very practised statesman. The Union entered the war with an advantage which the South did not possess, in an organized Government, which included War and Navy Departments. The military head of the former was General Scott, a Virginian who placed the cause of the Union above that of his State. He was a soldier of distinction, but was old in mind and body, and his intellect was no longer nimble enough[2] to enable him to cope with the crisis which confronted him. Naturally Lincoln leaned on him for military advice, and if at first the military measures of the Union were inadequate, much of the responsibility must rest with Scott. It was impossible, given the existing practice of the Constitution, — which required that contingents of troops, save those authorized by Congress for enlistment in the Federal forces,[3] should be found by and with the consent of the several States, — to apply conscription. With a people ignorant of war in general and of the nature of the particular struggle to which it was committed, this would have been in 1861 politically impossible if it had been otherwise feasible, while, even if there had been no constitutional or political obstacles, it would have been a useless measure, since the North could not have equipped a general levy. In his address on July 4, 1861, Lincoln said: "One of the greatest perplexities of the Government is to avoid receiving troops faster than it can provide for them" — a perplexity with which Kitchener was faced in 1914, and one which must confront every statesman and soldier suddenly called upon to develop national strength for war, if measures for that development have not been prepared systematically beforehand.

But if it was useless to summon larger numbers at first, a serious blunder was made in limiting the service of the. first 75,000 volunteers to three months. It is remarkable that Scott, whose operations in Mexico had been hampered by the expiration of the service of his volunteers, should not have seen this and told the President that civilians could not be made into soldiers in that time. Lincoln, who had a clearer idea than most of his advisers of the nature of the war, was, within a month of his first call, asking for volunteers for three years, but it was then too late to change the terms of the first contingent.

A charge from which it is more difficult to defend the President is that he gave way to the popular clamor that something should be done, and insisted that these three-months volunteers should be sent before their term expired to attack the Confederate position at Manassas in the first battle of Bull Run. So one mistake led to another, and the first battle of the war was lost. The Federal general in command in that battle was a competent soldier[4] and his plans were good, but his men were, from lack of training and discipline, incapable of executing them.

Lincoln's answer to the defeat of Bull Run was a call for 500,000 volunteers for three years, and an exercise of certain of his Presidential powers which caused many Senators and Congressmen to make wry faces. He also brought General

McClellan from Western Virginia, where he had gained a substantial success, to command the troops around Washington. McClellan was then thirty-nine years old. He had been an officer of the Engineers in the United States Army and had served with credit on General Scott's staff during the Mexican War. On leaving the army, he had been first chief engineer and then vice-president of the Central Illinois Railway. While in that position he had taken a keen interest in politics, and had been an active supporter of Douglas, Lincoln's chief political opponent. This was one of the causes of his undoing. Not that there is the smallest evidence that McClellan's political views ever influenced Lincoln's attitude towards his general, but it did not make McClellan very favorably disposed towards Lincoln, and it was the cause of suspicion and distrust in certain members of Lincoln's entourage. Thus there were, from the first, seeds of trouble which quickly germinated and grew.

McClellan was undoubtedly a good soldier. Lee after the war declared that of the Union generals the ablest was "McClellan by long odds";[5] but Lee knew McClellan only as an opponent. Grant also after the war declared: "If McClellan had gone into

war as Sherman, Thomas, or Meade, had fought
his way along and up, I have no reason to suppose
he would not have won as high distinction as
any of us."[6] Grant had opportunity of knowing of
McClellan's performances both as a commander of
troops in the field and as a commander-in-chief in
relations with a Government, and his judgment is
probably the more correct of the two.

GEORGE B. McCLELLAN

When McClellan was brought to Washington he was a young man of attractive manner and appearance; he had real gifts of organization and leadership, and was quickly not only respected but loved by his men. He became the idol of the press, which dubbed him the 'Young Napoleon" — a nickname not without reference to his habit of issuing somewhat flamboyant proclamations to his troops. Everyone from the President downwards was anxious to serve and help him. As he wrote to his wife, "I find myself in a most strange position here, President, Cabinet, General Scott, all deferring to me. By some strange operation of magic I seem to have become a power in the land."[7] In October General Scott resigned, and Lincoln made McClellan Commander-in-Chief. All this seems to have turned the General's head. He was lacking in the elements of courtesy to the President, of whom the best he could say was, "'He is honest and means well,"[8] while admitting that Lincoln had gone out of his way to be civil to him. After the first enthusiasm for him had cooled there was a good deal of political intriguing against him, and McClellan, finding the difficulties which he had himself in great measure created becoming too much for him, classed, in his anger, all the administration in Washington as "unscrupulous and false."[9]

McClellan's organization of the army proceeded apace, and the public expectation of it and him were high. But time passed, the army did not move, and expectation changed first to impatience and then to outspoken criticism. On October 21 an ill-managed affair at Ball's Bluff, on the Potomac above Washington, ended in a disastrous repulse of the Federal troops. One of the results of this repulse was the establishment of a Congressional committee of inquiry, which developed into a committee on the conduct of the war. The proceedings of this committee were often injudicious, and they were periodically a thorn in Lincoln's side. Two of its principal members[10] were hostile to McClellan, and disposed to think that Lincoln was wanting in energy in the conduct of the war. Partly from this source and partly from other quarters, the pressure on the President for some definite military action increased. At first, Lincoln, remembering Bull Run, resisted the pressure and told McClellan, "You must not fight till you are ready."[11] Then in December McClellan fell ill and the critics held their peace till he recovered; but no sooner was he back at work than the pressure on the President was renewed with greater strength, and yielding to it, Lincoln did a very foolish thing. He assumed his power as Commander-in-Chief, and in that capacity issued three orders. The first, called "'The President's General War Order No. I,'" issued on January 27, fixed Washington's Birthday, February 22, 1862, as the day "'for a general advance by the land and naval forces of the United States,' and directed "that all forces both land and naval, with their commanders, obey existing orders for the time and be ready to obey additional orders when given.' The second order, issued on January 31, directed that McClellan's Army of the Potomac should, after providing for the safety of Washington, "be formed into an expedition for the immediate object of seizing and occupying a point upon the railroad southwestward of what is known as Manassas Junction." The third order, issued on March 8, stipulated "that no change of the base of operations of the Army of the Potomac be made without leaving in and about Washington such a force as in the opinion of the General-in-Chief and the commanders of army corps shall leave the said city entirely secure," and further stated that not more than half the army should be moved away from Washington "until the navigation of the Potomac... shall be freed from enemy's batteries."[12]

Now when political and military control are not

combined it is very necessary that the statesman should state clearly in writing to his commanders the objects for which they are to fight, and the military policy which they are to follow. This is of even greater importance for the statesman than it is for the soldiers, for any vagueness of policy is certain to have its effect upon the whole conduct of the war. Further, when the instructions of the Government to its generals are committed to writing, the soldiers have the opportunity of clearing up any doubts or of suggesting modifications in their instructions when and if changes of circumstances appear to make a revision of policy advisable. All this seems to be plain common sense, but it is a precaution which, as the history of war discloses, has been omitted more often than it has been observed. If Davis had cleared his mind by defining his military policy to his generals, many of his difficulties and uncertainties would have disappeared. In March 1915 Sir Ian Hamilton was sent out to the Dardanelles with nothing but vague and general instructions, and the uncertainty as to policy which this indicates was one of the causes of the failure of his unlucky enterprise.[13] A like lack of definite instructions, due to a similar vagueness of policy, had consequences almost as serious in the case of the expedition to Mesopotamia.

Lincoln was quite right to issue instructions to McClellan, but it is clear that none of his orders, except perhaps the third, was intended to be an instruction as to military policy. They were meant to arouse McClellan to action; they probably made him laugh, for the absurdity of ordering a general advance of all forces to take place on an anniversary four weeks ahead, without any consideration of what the enemy might do and what the weather might be, and the still greater absurdity of telling soldiers and sailors to be ready to obey orders, must have been as patent to himasit is to us.

Two years later Lincoln explained his strange action to Grant, who says: "'In my first interview with Lincoln alone, he stated to me that he had never professed to be a military man or to know how campaigns should be conducted, and never wanted to interfere in them, but that procrastination on the part of commanders and the pressure from the people of the North and Congress, which was always with him, forced him into issuing his 'Military Orders', one, two, three, etc. He did not know but they were all wrong, and did know that some of them were."[14] This being the matured opinion of their author, we need not dwell further on the form of these orders; but the cause of their issue is worth some consideration.

Scott had gone, and McClellan was, or should have been, Lincoln's military adviser. The General was in Washington and was given all possible encouragement by the President to be on friendly and confidential terms. He was not ignorant of the trend of popular opinion, and his political experience should have told him that a statesman in a democratic country has to have some ground for resisting the demands of press and parliament. Yet McClellan never made the least effort to take the President into his confidence.[15] He was quite tight to refuse to advance until he was ready, and prone though he was to be overcautious in preparation and to exaggerate the strength of his enemy, he cannot be said to have asked too much in requiring six months to train and organize the army which had been disrupted by the battle of Bull Run.

The first new divisions created by Kitchener began to land in France in April 1915, about seven months after the outbreak of war, and they first went into battle at Loos, five months later. The

first American divisions were engaged just a year
after the United States had entered the war. It is
true that the Germans created after the outbreak
of war four new army corps, and engaged them
in the first battle of Ypres within three months
of the beginning of hostilities. This was a very
remarkable feat of organization; but the Germans
had resources, in trained officers and noncommis-
sioned officers, which neither Great Britain nor
the United States possessed, and the experiment
of employing these new levies so speedily was a
failure nearly as complete as that of McDowell's
men at Bull Run, for the gallant but ignorant
young German soldiers suffered terrible losses because of their lack of training and experience. The
time which McClellan, with the memory of Bull
Run in his mind, required cannot fairly be said to
have been excessive, even when every allowance is
made for the inexperience of the Southern troops,
and he knew what many other generals in the war
discovered later, that the state of Virginian roads
did not encourage campaigning in January and
February.

If McClellan had accepted the confidence which
was offered to him and had told Lincoln these

things, we may be reasonably certain, from our knowledge of the President's behavior later in the war, that he would have withstood popular pressure and supported his general through thick and thin. But left without information and means of reply to persistent critics, Lincoln was first perplexed and then perturbed, and if in that state of mind he did things which were militarily foolish, the chief cause of this was that his military adviser left him without military advice, while a secondary cause was a gap in the organization for conducting the war.

McClellan was at one and the same time the military adviser of the Government, in general command of all the Union forces, and in executive command of its main army. He could not fulfill all these functions. Lincoln had from the first and throughout the war a very definite military policy. He said that he made no pretense of being either a military leader or a financier, but he was enough of both to know that when a nation got into war, it must push the war with some vigor, or the nation would be demoralized and bankrupt.[16] He wanted the greatest possible military pressure brought to bear upon the South at the earliest possible moment, but he did not know how to translate this policy into suitable instructions to his generals. He required a military interpreter of his policy as well as a commander of his armies, and it took him some time to discover that need. McClellan's fault, like Johnston's, was that he did not know how to treat his political chief. It was this defect which was the main cause of the ruin of a promising campaign. I have always believed that McClellan's plan of transferring his army to the Yorktown peninsula was good. It made use of that factor in which the North was incontestably superior, sea power, and it brought the Army of the Potomac with little loss into a position before Richmond which Grant only attained after desperate and costly fighting. But McClellan made a fatal omission in framing his plan. One of the dominant considerations in the strategy of the war was the exposed position of the Federal capital on the Potomac. Lincoln had repeatedly and clearly expressed to McClellan his anxiety for the safety of Washington. He had urged that the army should make a direct advance upon Manassas because this would cover the capital, and had finally and with manifest reluctance agreed to McClellan's plan on the express condition that such a force of troops be left behind as would make the city "entirely secure."[17]

The one occasion on which McClellan made a serious attempt to take the Government into his confidence was on February 3, 1862, when he gave the Secretary of War a long and general description of his plans. This was in reply to a letter from Lincoln of this same date which ran:—

"If you will give satisfactory answers to the following questions, I shall gladly yield my plan to yours:

"1st. Does not your plan involve a greatly larger expenditure of time and money than mine?

"2nd. Wherein is a victory more certain by you plan than mine?

"3rd. Wherein is a victory more valuable by your plan than mine?

"4th. In fact, would it be less valuable in this: that it would break no great line of the enemy's communications, which mine would?

"5th. In case of disaster, would not a retreat be more difficult by your plan than by mine?"[18]

Of this letter it may be said that it was no part of Lincoln's business to have a military plan of his own. He should have said to McClellan: 'Such and such is the policy of the Government. How do you propose to execute it and at the same time provide for the safety of Northern territory, and in particular of Washington?' On receiving McClellan's reply, he would, if he was in any doubt, be justified in asking further questions to satisfy himself that the execution of the plan was likely to be within the means, financial and other, which the State could provide, and would fulfill the Government's conditions. If still unsatisfied, he should either have required a fresh plan to be prepared or have changed his general. In 1915 Great Britain was seriously hampered by the fact that more than one civilian minister had a plan of his own of which he became the enthusiastic advocate. The preparation of plans of campaign is a matter which must be left to the experts, who, in their turns, must satisfy their Governments that their plans are in agreement with the wishes and policy of those Governments. This means that statesmen and soldiers must have clear ideas as to their respective functions, and that there must be an established system of government in time of war by which civilian ministers are provided with the means of observing and checking the execution of their policy by their generals. Where no such system exists, the temptation to ministers to step outside their functions and become generals is often irresistible, and when not resisted, often fatal.

Whatever may be said of the remainder of Lincoln's orders, it was not merely his right but his duty to issue that part of the third order which dealt with the defense of Washington. Equally it was McClellan's duty, apart altogether from political consideration, of which he appears to have taken no account, to give on military grounds the utmost attention to the safety of his base. The number of troops agreed upon as necessary to make Washington ""entirely secure" was 35,000. It is unnecessary for us to go into the question whether McClellan did or did not leave that number, for that was only a part of his task. He should have come to an agreement as to the strength of the garrison with the general responsible for the defense of the capital, have discussed carefully with him the disposition of the troops, and the arrangement and arming of defensive works, and then, when he and the defender of Washington were in accord, he should have gone to the President and explained to him in detail how his instructions had been met, and what action would be taken to meet possible dangers. Instead he waited till he was actually on board ship and then sent to the Adjutant General in Washington a list of the troops left behind. General Wadsworth, chosen by Lincoln to command the defenses, immediately complained that he had not the numbers stated to be at his disposal. Thus from the outset the commander responsible for the safety of Washington was dissatisfied, and the President suspicious that his instructions had been evaded.

When Lee planned his brilliant campaign for the defense of Richmond he had no thought of using the small force in the Shenandoah Valley to attempt to capture Washington; the most that he required of Jackson in that respect was that after defeating Banks he should advance "towards the Potomac, and create the impression, as far as possible, that you design threatening that line."[19] The number of troops left behind by McClellan was quite sufficient to make Washington safe so long as the main Confederate army was occupied with the defense of Richmond; but Lee was aiming not at Washington but at the minds of the authorities in Washington, and McClellan played straight into his hands by leaving, when he embarked for the Yorktown peninsula, those minds very susceptible to alarm. How alarmed they were when Jackson hurled back "commissary Banks" and appeared at Winchester is notorious, but the prime cause of the foolish military measures which were the consequence of these alarms was less Lincoln's desire to interfere with strategy than McClellan's contempt for "the weakness and unfitness of the poor things who control the destinies of this great country,"[20] and the complete absence of harmony between the soldier and the statesman, for which in this case the soldier was the more responsible. Even before Banks's defeat had alarmed Washington, McClellan's neglect to satisfy Lincoln that the capital was secure had been the cause of serious derangement of the plan of attack upon Richmond, for the President on receiving a report from generals appointed to investigate the circumstances, to the effect that McClellan had not complied with his instructions, ordered that the First Corps under McDowell should not embark for the Peninsula, but remain in northeastern Virginia to cover Washington. McClellan was furious. ""It is," he wrote, "the most infamous thing that history has recorded . . . The idea of depriving a general of 35,000 troops when actually under fire."[21] These protestations do not alter the fact that McClellan's own conduct is Lincoln's justification. The soldier who expects the statesman to agree to expose the vitals of his country to danger, in reliance upon the doubtful issue of a battle to be fought at a distance from those vitals, is strangely ignorant of human nature, nor is it prudent to rely upon the statesman's power of resistance to the howl for protection which will surely follow any threat to those vitals. It was useless for McClellan to write to the President: ""We must beat the enemy in front of Richmond. One division added to this army for that effort would do more to protect Washington than his [McDowell's] whole force can possibly do anywhere else in the field."[22] That kind of argument is only of avail when the soldier has by his proved skill of generalship in the field won the complete confidence of statesmen and public, and that was far from being McClellan's position.

I have suggested that Davis was lacking in boldness in not taking troops from the coast to strengthen Johnston and enable him to invade

Maryland in the autumn of 1861, and in not increasing Lee's army for the campaign of Gettysburg in the spring of '63, but Davis's problem is hardly comparable to that of Lincoln in April '62, for in the first of these cases the Confederate President would have exposed nothing vital to the South, and in the second the confidence of his people in Lee would have assured him against political and popular pressure.

So far I have been defending Lincoln from some of the charges which are commonly made against him, but he did some things at this period which cannot be defended, and were — as he showed by his subsequent action that he realized — due to his ignorance of how to conduct war. He had appointed to command in the west Frémont, a politician of importance, with special influence among the more extreme abolitionists, but an incompetent soldier, and when McClellan was starting on his campaign against Richmond he detached a division from the Army of the Potomac and sent it to Frémont. For this the only possible defense is that he could not find at this period a competent soldier to advise how to answer political and popular pressure. When McClellan was preparing for his expedition Lincoln had relieved him of his position of Commander-in-Chief, thinking rightly enough that the Yorktown peninsula would not be a good place from which to direct all the military forces of the Union. Having lost much of his confidence in his soldiers, he appointed no one to take the place McClellan had held, and he made the same mistake as Davis in organizing his forces into military departments, and in seeking with the assistance of his War Secretary, Stanton, to coordinate their activities himself. This was the position when Jackson made his alarming advance down the Shenandoah Valley. Confronted with what they believed to be a great national emergency, and having no machinery to deal with it, Lincoln and Stanton took it upon themselves to devise maneuvers and combinations of troops which had little relation to the facts of the situation, and to issue military orders which were as bad of their kind as they well could be. The effect of these orders has been well summarized by Henderson as causing 175,000 men to be absolutely paralyzed by 16,000.[23] Lee in Richmond could hardly, if he had had the power for twenty-four hours of issuing orders to the Federal forces, have devised any arrangements more exactly suited to his needs.

The best that can be said for Lincoln's bungling in this business is that it was one of the consequences of McClellan's attitude towards him, and that he saw almost at once that he had blundered. His first orders to his generals to cut off Stonewall Jackson were issued on May 24. On June 26 Lincoln had abandoned the system of separate departments, — to which Davis clung till much later, — and appointed General Pope to command all the troops in Virginia and around Washington, with the exception of the Army of the Potomac. A fortnight later he summoned General Halleck to Washington to be Commander-in-Chief of the Union forces. Neither selection was fortunate, but both men had made some reputation for themselves in the west. Grant was under a cloud as the result of the battle of Shiloh, and Lincoln had had some ado to withstand pressure for his dismissal. It is therefore difficult to name anyone who on his reputation at this period of the war should have been preferred to these two. Lincoln at least reestablished a correct military hierarchy and organization; he could judge his generals only by putting them to the test of performance.

In the unfortunate wrangle that followed between Halleck and McClellan, the result of which was that the latter was successful neither in keeping a large force of Confederates in front of Richmond nor in giving timely help to Pope, Lincoln had no part. When Pope's army was defeated by Lee at the second battle of Bull Run and was retreating in rout upon Washington, McClellan had reached the capital. The President gave him first command of all the troops in and around Washington, and then merged the remnant of Pope's Army of Virginia in the Army of the Potomac, of which McClellan resumed the active leadership. In doing this Lincoln had to meet fierce opposition in his Cabinet, but, as he said of McClellan to his secretary, 'There is no man in the army who can man these fortifications and lick these troops of ours into shape half as well as he.'[24]

In view of the relations which existed between the two men, both acted finely. McClellan accepted his hard task without making any conditions, and wrote humbly, "I will do my best with God's help to perform it."[25] He set to work with a will, and in a remarkably short time so restored the discipline of the troops that within fifteen days of his resumption of the command they had fought on the Antietam one of the fiercest struggles of the war. That battle, it is true, was not distinguished by McClellan's generalship, but it at least forced Lee to retreat into Virginia, and McClellan was justified in claiming it as a victory. But success, even of a moderate kind, went to his head as power had done earlier. He wrote of a small preliminary action which preceded the battle: "If I can believe one tenth of what is reported, God has seldom given an army a greater victory than this."[26] And of the battle itself he said, with a return to his old self-complacency: "Those on whose judgment I rely tell me that I fought the battle splendidly and that it was a masterpiece of att.... I feel that I have done all-that can be asked in twice saving the country."[27] All that was asked was that he should follow up his victory; but he was convinced that his old regiments were completely tired out, the new not fit for the field, and it was not in his character to picture the enemy's troubles when he was faced with difficulties. Lee's far less numerous army was certainly the more weary of the two.

One result of the battle of the Antietam was the issue by Lincoln of his first Emancipation Proclamation. The measure was far from meeting with the approval of his Cabinet, which he endeavored to wheedle into a humor for its reception by reading one of his extracts from Artemus Ward. Nor was it at first received with any warmth of welcome by the people of the North. In the Army of the Potomac numbers of the soldiers desired to voice their objections by demonstration, but McClellan, who disapproved of it as strongly as anyone, loyally told them that the place for soldiers to express their political views was in the ballot box. None the less it was a political measure which had a great effect upon the conduct of the war, and the time chosen for taking it was opportune.[28]

After Fredericksburg and Chancellorsville the opinion began to be expressed in England that the North could not force the South into the Union and that the British Government should intervene. These expressions of opinion were answered by others still more pronounced from those whose hopes of abolition had been revived by Lincoln's Proclamation, and the strength of popular sympathy in Great Britain with the North became so clear that even during the excitement and friction aroused by the activities of the Alabama there was never any likelihood that the Government would depart from its attitude of neutrality. The Proclamation had settled the question of intervention, and ere long it gave the North a cause to fight for with enthusiasm, which rallied that far from insignificant body of persons who were doubtful whether it was right or expedient to maintain the Union by force of arms.[29]

With his mind cleared of this grave problem, Lincoln became more than ever eager that the war should be prosecuted with vigor. However, he curbed his impatience. He visited McClellan and his army early in October and was very friendly. "He told me," wrote McClellan, "he was convinced that I was the best general in the country."[30] But without help from the soldier the statesman could not keep that conviction. October passed and McClellan made no move, but during that month Jeb Stuart with the Confederate cavalry for the second time rode completely round his army — an event which gave McClellan's numerous enemies opportunities for derision, and was the signal for a renewal of political pressure upon Lincoln to have

him removed. On November 5, when McClellan
had not yet brought his army into contact with
Lee's, Lincoln finally yielded to the pressure and
replaced him by Burnside.

There can be little doubt but that McClellan was a far abler soldier than were his immediate successors, and at the time when he was removed he had at last completed to his satisfaction his somewhat meticulous preparations and had begun an advance with a definite plan of campaign in his mind. The moment chosen by Lincoln to make a change was therefore not a happy one. The immediate cause of McClellan's downfall was political animosity and the suspicion, which history has proved to have been unjust, that McClellan deliberately left Pope in the lurch; but the ultimate cause of this and of all McClellan's misfortunes was his incapacity to establish relations of trust and confidence with Lincoln. He never could free himself from the obsession that he and he alone was capable of conducting the war in all its aspects, and the many intrigues against him in Washington, of which it would appear from his correspondence that he had very complete information, tended to harden him in his opinion that all the politicians in Washington were dishonest schemers, and all the administrators incompetents. This was due in a great part to McClellan's character and mentality, but a little study on his part of how to deal with a statesman in war, and on Lincoln's part of the principles of statecraft in the conduct of war, would almost certainly have overcome such difficulties as existed and have enabled McClellan to be a very valuable servant of the State.

Notes:

1. France mobilized on August1. German cavalry crossed the Belgian frontier early on August 4, and the British order for mobilization was issued at 4 p.m. that same day.

2. None the less, Scott's plan of campaign for a concerted movement from north and west against the Confederacy was very similar to that eventually adopted by Grant. It was however rejected by McClellan, whose opinion of Scott was: "'The old General always comes in the way. He understands nothing; appreciates nothing."

3. Early in May Lincoln stretched his powers to the full by calling for an addition of 22,714 men to the Federal army and 18,000 to the Federal navy, in anticipation of the consent of Congress.

4. McDowell

5. Long: *Memoirs of Robert E. Lee*, p. 253.

6. Young: *Around the World with General Grant*, vol. Il, p. 217.

7. *McClellan's Own Story*, p- 91.

8. *Ibid.*, p. 176.

9. *Ibid.*

10. Wade and Chandler.

11. Hay: *Letters and Diary*, vol. I, p. 48.

12. *O. R.*, vol. V, p. 211 *ef seq.*

13. Sir Ian Hamilton: *Gallipoli Diary*, vol. 1, p. 15.

14. *Personal Memoirs of U. S. Grant*, p. 122.

15. He wrote, in November '61, "I am concealed at Stanton's to dodge all enemies in the shape of 'browsing' Presidents, etc." *McClellan's Own Story*, p. 176.

16. Barton: *Life of Lincoln*, vol. Il, p. 238.

17. *O. R.*; vol. V, p: 4.

18. *O. R.*, vol. V, p. 41.

19. *O. R.*, vol. XII, part 111, p. 892.

20. *McClellan's Own Story*, p. 175. 2 Ibid., p. 308.

21. *Ibid.*, p. 308.

22. *O.R.*, vol. XI, part 1, p. 29.

23. Henderson: *Stonewall Jackson*, vol. I, p. 508.

24. Hay: *Letters and Diary*, vol. 1, p. 64.

25. *McClellan's Own Story*, p. 566.

26. *Ibid.*, p. 612, written of the action at South Mountain.

27. *Ibid.*, p. 612.

28. Lincoln himself described it as "a military necessity absolutely essential for the preservation of the Union."

29. Greeley, who in 1860 declared, "Whenever a considerable section of our Union shall deliberately resolve to go out, we shall resist all coercive measures designed to keep it in," was telling the President in August '62 that "the Union cause has suffered and is now suffering immensely from your mistaken deference to rebel slavery."

30. *McClellan's Own Story*, p. 655.

4

Abraham Lincoln and Grant

THE public which gives its sons to fight is in time of war subjected to a novel and exhausting strain. Even the more phlegmatic Anglo-Saxon races tend in such times to become neurotic, and are apt to be aroused to enthusiasm or indignation on very slight grounds. This is one of the difficulties with which the statesmen of modern democracies must reckon. The experienced soldier knows how manifold are the chances and the uncertainties of war; how incomplete in normal circumstances is the information on which he has to make decisions; he is only too aware that with the highest skill and the best judgment he cannot hope to guess right all the time. It is the duty of the statesman to know this too, for the public does not read the maxims of Napoleon, and is not aware that the victory falls to the general who makes fewest mistakes; it judges by results and readily becomes intolerant of any error which has caused loss of life. The statesman who understands his business will stand between his soldiers and hasty popular judgment. Both Lincoln and Davis have it to their eternal credit that they did this, and prevented the outstanding military figures of the war from being swept by blasts of popular criticism into oblivion in the early days of the conflict.

We have seen that McClellan's easy success in Western Virginia caused the Northern public to hail him as a hero. The Southern public expected, when Lee was sent to the same theatre, that he would return with greater glory than had been won by the Northern general. It did not, it could not, know that Lee's problem was entirely different from McClellan's. Lee failed to obtain results, and therefore was condemned. So it happened that, while he was in the act of preparing those masterly combinations which saved Richmond,

Davis had to support him against the outspoken and sarcastic comments of the Southern press. In this case it happened that Davis knew Lee, and he backed his own judgment against that of the public, to find it triumphantly vindicated.

Lincoln had not had Davis's opportunities of becoming acquainted with the officers of the Army of the United States. He did not know Grant, and could judge of him only as the public did, by his performances in the field. On April 6, 1862 Grant made, at the battle of Shiloh, a blunder which could be retrieved only by a heavy sacrifice of life. Public feeling was immediately stirred. Stories of the failing which had caused his resignation from the army were revived, and it was even said, on no evidence at all, that he had been drunk during the battle. Lincoln was pressed to remove him; but the President remembered that at a time when his other generals were finding abundant reasons for inaction Grant had captured Forts Henry and Donelson, and that if he had made a mistake at Shiloh that mistake caused him not to retreat but to attack. His answer came pat to those who sought Grant's disgrace: "'I cannot spare this man. He fights."[1] As late as March 1863, when the remarkable campaign which ended in the fall of Vicksburg had begun, Grant was still being pilloried in the Northern press. His troops, struggling with the floods of the Mississippi, had a hard life. "Visitors to the camp," Grant tells us, "went home with dismal «stories to relate; Northern papers came back to the soldiers with the stories exaggerated. Because I would not divulge my ultimate plans to visitors, they pronounced me idle, incompetent, and unfit to command men in an emergency, and clamored for my removal."[2] Lincoln said at this time: "I think Grant has hardly a friend except myself."[3] He wanted a fighter, and believing that he had found such a one in General Grant, he stuck to him against all opposition. In May '63, before any decisive success had been won in the campaign for the control of the Mississippi, Lincoln had grasped what Grant was at, and had him informed that "he has the full confidence of the Government."[4] "With all the pressure brought to bear upon them," Grant writes, "both President Lincoln and General Halleck stood by me to the end of the campaign. I had never met Mr. Lincoln, but his support was constant."[5]

Such should be, but too often is not, an

invariable rule with statesmen in their relations with commanders in the field. The generals must be supported, or removed. To keep them in command when they have evidence that they are distrusted at home is to place upon them a burden which may break them, or will certainly make it harder for them to win victories. Yet in 1917 we find the French Government, on the eve of a great campaign, making it evident to their commander, General Nivelle, that they had no confidence in his plans, while retaining him in military control and directing him to proceed with his battle.

The story of Lincoln's early relations with Grant is evidence that it was no eagerness on the President's part to do the work of his general, or any dislike of soldiers as a class, which brought about the friction between himself and McClellan.

Neither Lincoln's support nor the triumph of Vicksburg made Grant a popular hero. The critics had been too recently vocal upon one note to change enthusiastically to another. Indeed, few at the time realized the full significance of Vicksburg and of Gettysburg. The memories of Fredericksburg and Chancellorsville were too fresh to let men rejoice without fear of some early disillusionment.

But when in November '63 Grant put energy and decision into the halting operations of the Union Forces in Tennessee and won the victory of Chattanooga, the first genuine Thanksgiving since the outbreak of the Civil War was made possible, and the North realized that it had found a man.[6] The rank of Lieutenant General was revived for Grant, and he was summoned to Washington to be Commander-in-Chief of the Union forces.

A part of Grant's account of his first interview with the President I have already quoted. The remainder is not of less interest. Lincoln, he says, told him: "'All he wanted or had ever wanted was someone who would take responsibility and act, and call on him for all the assistance he needed, pledging himself to use all the power of the Government in rendering such assistance. . . . The President told me he did not want to know what I proposed to do."[7] It needed some severe self-control on Lincoln's part to say that. He had formed the habit of going daily to the War Department and there studying the latest telegrams and the maps with the positions of the troops marked; he had taken to reading books on strategy, and had been accustomed to make suggestions for their military movements to his generals. His brain was of that not uncommon type which finds delight in the intellectual exercise of framing military plans. Even now, when he had found his man and given him his complete confidence, he could not resist the temptation to produce a plan of campaign. "He submitted," Grant goes on, "a plan of campaign of his own, which he wanted me to hear and then do as I pleased about. He brought out a map of Virginia on which he had evidently marked every position occupied by the Federal and Confederate armies up to that time. He pointed out on the map two streams which empty into the Potomac, and suggested that the army might be moved on boats and landed between the mouths of these streams. We would then have the Potomac to bring out supplies and the tributaries would protect our flanks while we moved out. I listened respectfully, but did not suggest that the same streams would protect Lee's flanks while he was shutting us up."[8] That little story should be on the desk of every minister who finds himself in office during war.

When Grant assumed the chief control of the Union forces, effective unity of command was for the first time achieved in the North. He planned a great campaign against the Confederacy from the north, from the west, and from the coast, and decided to accompany himself the Army of the Potomac commanded by Meade, in its operations against Lee's Army of Northern Virginia. By thus keeping his most formidable opponent under his eye, and by selecting for the Army of the Potomac a line of advance which he believed would sufficiently cover the capital, while the Shenandoah Valley was controlled by another force of Federal troops, he allayed the anxieties for the safety of Washington which had proved the undoing of others. Halleck became Chief of Staff and remained in Washington to act as the channel of communication between Grant and the Government, and the interpreter of the soldier's military language. This arrangement, come to early in 1864, was not merely practical and sensible — it was ahead of any system for the conduct of war which had been devised in Europe until von Moltke in 1866 and 1870 displayed the Prussian methods to an astonished military world.

The encouragement which Lincoln had given Grant when the soldier was in the west naturally tended to make relations between them easy when they met. But apart from this, Grant was exactly fitted by character and mentality to cooperate with the President. He had not Lee's extraordinary skill in maneuver, but he had the vision to see the military problem of the Union as a whole, the imagination to draw his plans on a big scale, the courage to stick to his plans in adversity, and a real understanding of the responsibilities and anxieties of the Government. He was not a talker, though he could express his ideas on paper clearly and succinctly; he was a man of action, who thought before acting and knew his own mind; and that was the type of man for whom Lincoln had been seeking. "You are vigilant and self-reliant," wrote the President to him soon after Grant had taken the field; "and, pleased with this, I wish not to obtrude any restraints or constraints upon you... . If there be anything wanting in my power to give do not fail to let me know. And now with a brave army and a just cause, may God sustain you.'"

The pages of the *Official Records* are a clear indication of the change which Grant's appointment made in the conduct of the war. Until the Lieutenant General entered upon his functions the correspondence between Lincoln and his generals had been frequent and voluminous. On the part of the soldiers it often consisted of complaints of the inefficiency of the administration or of requests for guidance upon matters which they should have decided for themselves. On Lincoln's part it comprised too frequently suggestions for military manoeuvres forced from him because his generals showed doubts and hesitations. From March 1864 all this ceased. The bulk of Grant's correspondence was addressed to Halleck; he and the President rarely exchanged letters, and the latter, relieved from many worries and perplexities, became definitely master of his house. Grant took an early opportunity of assuring the powers in Washington of his gratitude for their zeal in supplying his needs — a pleasing change from the usual tenor of correspondence from the army. Soldier and statesman set about their business without interfering each with the other, and consequently the work of both prospered.

ULYSSES S. GRANT

This does not mean that Lincoln handed over
to another his responsibility for the conduct of
the war. The statesman cannot divest himself of

such responsibility, and Lincoln made no attempt to do so. He read every line of Grant's reports, and followed all his movements with the closest attention. Grant's plan was to combine all the forces of the Union, naval and military, east and west, in one great coordinated effort, and with these forces "to hammer continuously against the armed force of the enemy and his resources until by mere attrition if in no other way there should be nothing left to him but an equal submission with the loyal section of our community to the Constitutional laws of the land."[9] The Northern forces were to work together with one object, that object being to deprive the centrally placed enemy of his chief weapon, maneuver, by fastening on to each of his armies and compelling them to fight often and to fight hard. Some of the details of the execution of this plan may be criticized as lacking in finesse and as causing avoidable loss of life, but it gave to the Union forces a definite goal and a precise purpose for their efforts which had been lacking heretofore, and it was the simplest method of bringing the superior military power of the North into play.

Grant's appointment had been hailed with enthusiasm in the North, and the hopes which it aroused ran high. The appearance of a new commander in war is generally the signal for an outburst of popular acclamation. But a public always greedy for results quickly becomes impatient if it does not get them, and impatience is apt to change to disappointment and anger. When Grant's eagerly expected advance began and was followed by the long lists of casualties from the battlefields of the Wilderness, Spottsylvania, and Cold Harbor, grief produced anxieties which turned to grumblings against the new Commander-in-Chief. These grumblings had their political reactions which, with the approach of the presidential election, were of importance. On July 2, 1864 Congress moved the President to appoint a day of humiliation and prayer. The situation was indeed not unlike that which in 1916 followed the close of the battle of the Somme. That great battle, the first in which the British Empire was engaged as a whole, brought mourning into thousands of homes, and opened the eyes of the British public to the cost of a struggle for national existence. In return for the terrible price paid, the gains which the map showed appeared insignificant, and the exhaustion of the German armies, which

Ludendorff has since disclosed to us,[10] was unknown to the citizen if it was more than suspected by the soldiers. It is not surprising in the circumstances that the Allied statesmen wavered in their confidence in their generals, and determined to have "'no more Sommes"; but we, with the recent memory of those days in our minds, may the more admire Lincoln's firmness and constancy.

A few days after the ill-planned and costly assault at Cold Harbor he told Grant: "I have just read your dispatch. I begin to see it. You will succeed. God bless you all."[11] Here was a reinforcement to Grant worth many thousands of men. Lincoln, having made up his mind to keep Grant, supported him when he most needed support; he saw that Grant was wearing out Lee's army and holding to it so tight that it could not maneuver, and told him that he both understood and approved. Two months later, August 16, 1864, when Grant's assaults upon Lee's lines at Petersburg had failed, when despondency in the North had again become general, and the demands for a peace of accommodation were increasing, Lincoln again wrote: "I have seen your dispatch expressing your unwillingness to break your hold where you are.

Neither am I willing. Hold on with a bulldog grip, and chew and choke as much as possible."[12]

This message, which gave Grant as clear an endorsement of his policy as any soldier could desire, is the more remarkable in that it followed on a mistake of Grant's which might well have shaken the President's confidence in him, and was sent at a time when Lincoln's political difficulties were probably greater than they were at any other period of the war.

When Grant moved the Army of the Potomac across the James to the siege of Petersburg, he was no longer well placed to supervise and direct the other forces of the Union. He had left a force in the Shenandoah Valley to block that favorite line of Confederate invasion, but this force, unskillfully handled, had been maneuver in the middle of June out of the Valley by a Confederate contingent under Early, who promptly marched for the Potomac, crossed it, and moved on Washington, arriving before the capital on July 11. Now Early's force was far more formidable than Jackson's which had created such alarm two years before, and the garrison of Washington in July 1864 was far more weak than that which McClellan had left when he sailed for the Yorktown peninsula. Yet the contrast of the effect in Washington of Early's and Jackson's raids is remarkable. Grant had, of course, been informed of Early's progress and had dispatched troops to cover Washington, but the information had come to him somewhat tardily, and the troops had not arrived when Early was in Maryland and within a day's march of the scantily garrisoned forts covering the capital. In spite of this there were none of the hectic and ill-considered orders which Lincoln and Stanton had showered upon their perplexed generals in 1862. Instead, we find Lincoln telegraphing to Grant on July 10: "General Halleck says we have absolutely no force here fit to go to the field. He thinks that, with the 1oo-days men and the invalids we have here, we cannot defend Washington and scarcely Baltimore. . . . Now that I think is that you should provide to retain your hold where you are certainly, and bring the rest with you personally, and make a vigorous effort to destroy the enemy's forces in this vicinity. I think there is really a big chance to do this if the movement is prompt. This is what I think upon your suggestion, and is not an order."[13]

The calls upon Lincoln for help against the bold raider came from all parts of Maryland and of Pennsylvania in '64 as they had in '62, but they were very differently answered. Here is his reply to one urgent appeal for troops: "I have not a single soldier but who is being disposed by the military for the best protection of all. By latest accounts the enemy is moving on Washington. Let us be vigilant, but keep cool. I hope neither Washington nor Baltimore will fall."[14] Neither Washington nor Baltimore fell, though it is possible that Early might have been able on July 11 to get some troops into the capital for a few hours. Actually he retreated on learning that the transports with Grant's troops had arrived off Washington. Grant well knew that the reinforcements he had sent would be ample to drive Early back, and he knew, too, that the purpose of the raid was to cause him to weaken his pressure on Petersburg. Therefore he replied to the President's suggestion that he should come himself to Washington with more troops: "I think, on reflection, it would have a bad effect for me to leave here."[15] Lincoln accepted that decision without question, and that acceptance — and indeed the whole incident — displays his implicit confidence in Grant, a confidence due not to blind trust but to the effect upon Lincoln's mind of close and continuous observation of the soldier's methods and actions. Most of Lincoln's correspondence with Grant begins with the words, "I have seen," or, "'I have read your dispatch,' and as proof that very little escaped the President's eye it may be mentioned that once when during the siege of Petersburg the usual supply of Richmond newspapers did not reach Washington, Lincoln promptly telegraphed to know the reason for the intermission. Grant was well aware that there was in Washington one ready to support him when he needed help, to give him a hand if he tripped, to remove him if he failed. Lincoln left Grant to his task, but he did not leave him without control and assistance.

Early's raid, which might under a looser system of conducting war have saved Richmond, as it was saved in '62, had no military results for the Confederacy save the material and supplies which he captured, and this was due to the relations Lincoln had established with his Commander-in-Chief. In fact the one serious military consequence of the raid was Grant's determination to close finally the famous covered way from Virginia into Maryland, which had so vexed his predecessors and eventually himself. For that purpose, and at Lincoln's instigation, he personally supervised the preparation of Sheridan's expedition, which not only prevented the Confederates from again using the Valley as a means of relieving the dangers to Richmond, but deprived Lee's army in the lines of Petersburg of its most convenient granary.

I have said that Grant personally directed the preparation for the last campaign in the Shenandoah Valley at Lincoln's instigation. He had told Halleck from his headquarters before Petersburg what he wanted done, and on reading this communication Lincoln at once telegraphed to him: "I have seen your dispatch in which you say, 'I want Sheridan put in command of all the troops in the field with instructions to put himself south of the enemy and follow him to the death. Where-ever the enemy goes let our troops go also.' This I think but . . . I repeat to you that it will not be done nor attempted unless you watch it every day and hour and force it.'"[16] Promptly came the answer, "I start in two hours for Washington,'" and Sheridan was started on his enterprise.

The sequel showed how truly Lincoln had sized up the situation and the men around him. One visit from Grant did not suffice, for the cautious Halleck and the nervous Stanton were holding Sheridan's ardor in chains. Grant gives us an account of this second visit: "On the 15th of September I started to visit General Sheridan in the Shenandoah Valley. My purpose was to have him attack Early and drive him out of the Valley and destroy that source of supplies for Lee's army. I knew that it was impossible for me to get orders through Washington to Sheridan to make a move, because they would be stopped there, and such orders as Halleck's caution (and that of the Secretary of War) would suggest would be given in-. stead. ... When Sheridan arrived I asked him if he had a map showing the positions of his army and that of the enemy. He at once drew one out of his pocket, showing all roads and streams and the camps of the two armies. He said that if he had permission he could move so and so (pointing out how) and he could 'whip them.'. . . I asked him if he could be ready to get off by the following Tuesday. This was on Friday. 'Oh yes,' he said, he 'could be off before daylight on Monday.' I told him then to make the attack at that time and according to his plan." Again we see the fallacy of supposing that Lincoln left Grant entirely to himself. Sheridan's Valley campaign was due primarily to his initiative and judgment. He no longer intervened as he had done in May '62; he had learned how to intervene wisely and opportunely.

But I must return to the message of August 16, telling Grant to play the bulldog. If the one military result of Early's raid was to bring Sheridan down upon him, it had serious political consequences. The appearance of Confederate troops nearer to Washington than they had ever been before, and in more formidable guise, caused many in the North to despair of victory.

The *New York World*, which had been exceptionally friendly to the Commander-in-Chief, asked on July 11, "Who shall revive the withered hopes that bloomed on the opening of Grant's campaign?" And nine days before, Congress had invited the President to appoint a day for national prayer and humiliation.

Horace Greeley attempted to open negotiations for peace by meeting Confederate Commissioners at Niagara, and in the middle of July two other semiofficial seekers for peace, James F. Jacques and J. R. Gilmour, had gone to Richmond, only to be told by the Southern President, "If your papers tell the truth, it is your capital that is in danger, not ours. . . . In a military view I should certainly say our position is better than yours." Greeley, despite the failure of his journey to Niagara, resumed his efforts to end the war, and on August 9 wrote to the President: "Nine tenths of the whole American people, North and South, are anxious for peace — peace on almost any terms, and utterly sick of human slaughter and devastation. . . . I beg you, implore you, to inaugurate or invite proposals for peace forthwith. And in case peace cannot now be made, consent to an armistice of one year, each party to retain unmolested all it now holds, but the rebel ports to be opened.'"

Not only was there this pressure from outside, there was discord within. Chase had resigned. A presidential election was drawing near, and there were outspoken predictions of a Republican defeat. The North was feeling as it had never felt before the strain of a prolonged conflict, and the nerves even of the most constant were a-twitter, while, as a culmination of Lincoln's political perplexities, the rumblings of opposition to the draft, which had just become law, were growing daily louder. If ever a harassed statesman was justified in asking his generals to do something which would help him in his political trials, surely Lincoln would have been justified in so doing in August 1864.

But what happened? Early in August the grumblings against the draft had alarmed Halleck, and on the eleventh of that month he told Grant: "Pretty strong evidence is accumulating that there is a combination formed or forming to make a forcible resistance to the draft in New York, Pennsylvania, Indiana, Kentucky, and perhaps some of the other States. The draft must be enforced, for otherwise the army cannot be kept up. But to enforce it may require the withdrawal of a considerable number of troops from the field. This possible, and I think very probable, exigency must be provided for." Four days later, on the evening of August 15, Grant answered from the lines before Petersburg: "If there is any danger of an uprising in the North to resist the draft or for any other purpose, our loyal governors ought to organize the militia at once to resist it. If we are to draw troops from the field to keep the loyal States in harness, it will prove difficult to suppress the rebellion in the disloyal States. My withdrawal from the James River would mean the defeat of Sherman.'"

This message from Grant is endorsed as received in Halleck's office in Washington at 7 a.m. on the seventeenth. We can picture the President taking his usual morning stroll after breakfast from the White House across to the War Department, and, on arriving in Halleck's room, asking for any messages from Grant. That of the fifteenth is handed to him, and he is told that it has just come in. He would naturally ask to see the dispatch which had evoked this reply. When he had read both messages, he must at once have scribbled the answer: "Hold on with a bulldog grip and chew and choke as much as possible." This telegram is marked as being dispatched at 10 A.M. on the seventeenth, that is, three and a half hours after Grant's dispatch reached the War Department. When we allow time for the ordinary routine of a large office, it is clear that there cannot have been the smallest hesitation in preparing it. And what does it mean? It says to Grant, in the first place, 'Go ahead with your job. I will look after the rear'; and it says further: "'I told you a few weeks ago that

I had begun to see it. Now I say more. Your policy is absolutely right. Hold on to Lee like a bulldog. Wear him out. Don't worry about anything else. I'll see you through." Was there ever a finer example of political courage? The process of wearing down the enemy must of necessity be tedious and costly; it would not provide any such quick and dramatic success as would raise the drooping spirits in the North and give a favorable turn to a doubtful political situation. Lincoln's answer gave Grant just the reinforcement he needed, and was a firm decision that what was militarily right should be done, without regard to what was or might appear to be politically expedient.

It is curious that the full meaning of this remarkable example of Lincoln's intervention in military affairs seems to have escaped most of the historians and biographers. Rhodes, for example, quotes it as an example of "Lincoln's eager desire for military success." Well, we know now that the slow processes of trench warfare are not such as to give the kind of military success which sets the bells ringing and the people cheering, and I believe that Lincoln knew it too when he wrote his message. The methods of the bulldog are sure, but they are neither speedy nor showy. In this case the President had not long to wait for the reward of his constancy. Within three weeks of his telling Grant to hold on, Sherman had entered Atlanta, and within five weeks Sheridan had twice defeated Early in the Valley, at Winchester and Fisher's Mill. On September 3 Lincoln was able to reply to the demand which Congress had made two months earlier for a day of humiliation, by calling for a day of thanksgiving for the victories of Farragut and Sherman — victories which had resolved political doubts and made his reélection certain.

But even when the success of Grant's combinations against the Confederacy was becoming patent to the most pessimistic, Lincoln continued to watch his general as carefully as he had when fortune seemed to be withholding her smiles. I could furnish many proofs of this, but will be content with one more. In February 1865 Sheridan had completed his task of clearing the Shenandoah Valley and Grant wanted his cavalry to move towards Richmond and help in the process of gradually overlapping Lee's lines around Petersburg. A part only of this correspondence appears

to have been seen by Lincoln, and that part an-
nounced Sheridan's departure from the Valley. On
February 25. the President telegraphed to Grant:
'General Sheridan's dispatch to you of to-day, in
which he says he 'will be off on Monday' and that
he will have behind him about 3000 men, causes
the Secretary of War and myself considerable
anxiety. Have you considered whether you do not
again leave open the Shenandoah Valley entrance
to Maryland and Pennsylvania, or at least to the
Baltimore & Ohio Railroad?" Grant's answer explained that Sheridan was referring to his cavalry
only, and that ample troops had been left to close
the Valley entrance to Northern territory; and this
message actually crossed another from Lincoln,
saying that he had discovered Sheridan's meaning, and apologizing to Grant for having troubled
him.[17] This little incident, due to a misinterpreta-
tion of correspondence speedily rectified and tri-
fling in itself, shows at least that Grant was under
no illusion that even the smallest of his actions
were unobserved, and while he had every reason
to be confident that the President would not interfere with his military functions, he knew that he

might at any moment be asked to explain either a commission or an omission.

It was not only in his correspondence with Grant that Lincoln showed how nicely he appreciated the functions of the civil and military powers in war. As the hold of the Union upon Southern territory grew firmer, attempts were made to organize some form of government in the occupied territory. Certain of the Northern generals found themselves in difficulties when confronted by the — to them — unwonted task of reconciling military necessities with civil government. In August 1864 General Butler proposed to settle such difficulties with the inhabitants by taking a popular vote. Lincoln promptly wrote him: "Nothing justifies the suspending of the civil by the military authority but military necessity, and of the existence of that necessity the military commander and not a popular vote is to decide. Whatever is not within that necessity must be left undisturbed."'

JUBAL A. EARLY
PHILIP H. SHERIDAN

Similar problems arose in western Mississippi when General Curly was in command. To him Lincoln wrote: 'I do not wish either cotton or the new State Government to take precedence of the military while the necessity for the military remains, but there is strong public reason for treating both with so much favor as may not be substantially detrimental to the military."[18] Lincoln had in fact worked out a definite formula for the relations between statesmen and soldiers in a democracy at war, and that formula has not since been improved. That he was fully conscious of the dangers of an excessive exercise of his dictatorial powers and of the necessity of adjusting to a nicety the claims of military necessity and of popular control is shown by a little speech which he made on November 10, 1864, two days after his reélection to the presidency, to a party of supporters who had come to serenade him. "It has long been a grave question, whether any Government not too strong for the liberties of its people can be strong enough to maintain its own existence in great emergencies. On this point the present rebellion brought our republic to a severe test and a presidential election added not a little to the strain.... In any future great national trial, compared with the men of this we shall have as weak and as strong, as silly and as wise, as bad and as good. Let us therefore study the incidents of this as philosophy to learn wisdom from, and none of them as wrongs to avenge."[19] It is in the belief that "the incidents of this" may still be studied as philosophy to learn wisdom from that I have delivered these lectures.

Before I say good-bye to Lincoln and Grant, I must give a last example to show how clear was the line which the President had drawn in his mind between the functions of policy and of strategy. In the last days of February 1865 the agony of the Confederacy was nigh and there were suggestions for a conference between Lee and Grant, with the object of making a settlement. Grant applied to Washington for instructions and the answer came from the War Secretary, but it had been drafted by Lincoln himself: "The President directs me to say to you that he wishes you to have no conference with General Lee unless it be for the capitulation of General Lee's army, or on some minor and ~ purely military matter. He instructs me to say that you are not to decide, discuss, or confer upon any political question. Such questions the President holds in his own hands, and will entrust them to no military conferences or conventions."[20]

When that famous meeting between Lee and Grant took place at Appomattox Court House, - Lincoln made no attempt to dictate to Grant the terms of surrender to be imposed upon the Army of Northern Virginia, that being a "purely military matter.' But it is hard to believe that Grant's noble generosity was not inspired by those yet more noble words with which just a month before Lincoln had closed his second Inaugural Address: "With malice toward none, with charity for all; with firmness in the right, as God gives us to see the right; let us strive on to finish the work we ate in, to bind up the nation's wounds; to cate for him who shall have borne the battle, and for his widow, and his orphan — to do all which may achieve and cherish a just and lasting peace amongst ourselves and with all nations."

Notes:

1. Rhodes: *History of the United States*, vol. II, p. 62.

2. *Personal Memoirs of U. S. Grant*, vol. II, p. 458.

3. Nicolay: *Personal Traits of Lincoln*, p. 253.

4. *O. R.*, vol. XXIV, part 1, p. 84.

5. *Personal Memoirs*, p. 460.

6. Rhodes: *History of the Civil War*, p. 299.

7. *Personal Memoirs*, p. 123.

8. *Personal Memoirs*, p. 123.

9. *O.R.*, vol. XXXVI, part 1, p. 13.

10. Ludendorff: *My War Memories*, vol. 1, pp.
266 *ef seq.*

11. *O.R.*, vol. XL, part m, p. 47.

12. *Ibid.*, XLII, part nu, p. 243.

13. *O. R.*, vol. XXXVII, part 1, p. 155.

14. *Ibid.*, p. 173.

15. *Ibid.*, p. 156.

16. *Ibid.*, p. 583.

17. *O. R.*, vol. XLVI, part n, p. 685.

18. Nicolay and Hay: *Abrabam Lincoln*, vol. VIII,
p. 448.

19. *Ibid.*, p. 380.

20. *O. R.*, vol. XLVI, part 1, p. 802.

5

——

A System for the Conduct of War

(A) The Need for a System

WE have now examined the relations which existed between two statesmen and four soldiers, during a great war under democratic systems of government. They have been examined frankly in the light of our own experience, and not in that of the experience and knowledge of war prevailing in the sixties of the last century. What are we to learn for our own advantage from the successes and failures of these men? The first lesson is, I think, obvious. Any Government which hopes to wage war successfully and without undue cost must have established, before arms clash, a well-considered system of conducting war. Lincoln, as we have seen, built up such a system under the stress of bitter experience. Davis, starting on his task with a far greater technical equipment than Lincoln possessed, never devised any effective system.

It is commonly said by students of the history of the American Civil War that Lincoln was from the first seeking for a man, and that when he had found a man in Grant the rest was easy. Those who take this view are apt to quote Napoleon: "In war men are nothing; it is the man who is everything. The general is the head, the whole of the army. It was not the Roman army that conquered Gaul, but Caesar; it was not the Carthaginian army that made Rome tremble in her gates, but Hannibal.'"

True enough of armies, but not the complete truth of modern nations at war. Sir William Robertson, who was the responsible adviser of a Government longer than any other soldier in the Great War, has said that the part of the effort of the British Empire for which he was responsible to the Cabinet was but twenty-five per cent of the whole.[1] There must, then, be someone to direct that whole and to coordinate its parts. It is not sufficient for the statesmen to choose leaders for armies, navies, and air forces, and to say to them, "'Now go and fight.'" I hope to have shown that that was not Lincoln's attitude to Grant. There must be direction — and constant direction — of strategy, but if direction is not to become mischievous interference the director must know how to direct. Here is the main difficulty which democracy must overcome if it is to be successful in war. Ministers who owe their position to votes have in time of peace more than sufficient to occupy them in meeting the daily needs and demands of voters. But voters in the mass take an interest in preparation for war only spasmodically, when they are alarmed, and then only in the provision of men and material, never in the organization of a system for the conduct of war. Ministers are therefore under no pressure to prepare themselves for a danger which mercifully is exceptional.

On the outbreak of the Great War our fleet and our small army were as well prepared as we can reasonably expect to find them in another like case. The Committee of Imperial Defense had elaborated a Wart Book which set forth the emergency legislation needed and the action required of every government department. All this stood well the test of experience. But no one had thought out the most important preparation of all, a system for the conduct of war. The Field Service Regulations, the soldier's bible in war, did indeed make in very general terms a brief statement of the respective functions of soldier and statesman in war, but I much doubt if they were read by any minister. So we entered upon the war with no system for its conduct, and had to pay the price of neglect, notably in the Dardanelles campaign. More than fifty years after Lincoln we had, like him, to rough out a system as the result of bitter experience, and at the cost of vast expenditure of blood and treasure; and it may be questioned if in the end our system was as good as his.

It is this lack of system, as I have said, and not any defect in the British Constitution, which was the cause of the weakness deplored by Lord Salisbury. Von Moltke designed for the autocratic Government of Prussia a method of conducting war which had great merits, but had one vital defect. Democracy can, if it will, devise a better.

Modern war demands, not Napoleon's man, but a partnership between the statesman and his military commanders.

I use the term "military" in its widest sense, to include all armed forces. The statesman must be the senior partner, and if the partnership is to be effective its members must have confidence each in the other, must be sufficiently acquainted with the whole business to understand the needs and difficulties of each, and the senior partner must know when and how to leave his fellows to their tasks — how to direct without interference. It requires no great effort to achieve this knowledge. For the statesman it demands no technical study of the details of strategy or of tactics — indeed, knowledge of this kind may be, in fact probably will be, positively harmful. We have seen how his military experience induced Davis to take upon himself functions which he should never have assumed, and to concern himself with details which should never have troubled him. We have seen how Lincoln's study of military books led him to make suggestions to his general of which few were opportune, and how his experience of war taught him to abandon such practices. But if the partnership is to be effective the statesman must have learned from the experience of others, as recorded in history, what are the essentials of a good system for conducting war and, having learned that, must have such a system ready before the time comes to put it to the test.

Further, if the partners are to work together the system must be known to all. Only when that is so can the military partners study their functions and determine their conduct. Neither J. E. Johnston nor McClellan had thought out the respective duties of soldier and statesman in time of war; they had not considered what the statesman should or should not be told. McClellan in | particular conceived that the one business of the President was to meet his demands, and neither soldier had any real understanding of the problems of his political chief. The result was such friction as gravely prejudiced the military operations of both sides —and instances of such friction are not confined to the Civil War. If the junior partners are to do their business they must know on what principles and by what methods their senior will act.

The difficulties in the past have arisen mainly because of a misconception of what is meant by the conduct of war. This has generally been supposed to mean the direction of armies and navies, and therefore a matter to be left to soldiers and sailors. To-day at least we should be aware that it means the direction for a special purpose of the whole power and resources of the nation. This is clearly not a matter to be left to soldiers or sailors, nor would any responsible soldier or sailor desire it to be so left. But it is a matter which requires preparation and organization as complete and systematic as does the mobilization of armed forces. It is a form of preparation which has the outstanding merit of costing nothing but thought, and of conveying no menace to a possible foe. The only difficulty in the way of getting it set on foot is the difficulty of getting the voters, who supply to ministers the inducement to act, interested in the subject. It is curious that, while most young men who aspire to take a part in public life make some study of social problems and methods of removing the evils from which the community suffers in time of peace, few if any make a study of how to deal with the greatest evil of all — war.

First in importance comes the study of the means of preventing war; but until those means have been found so certainly as to make war impossible, then surely a study of the means of conducting wat with the greatest success and with the least loss must come next. This is a study not without interest, for it brings one into touch with men acting in positions of great responsibility under great stress, and it is certainly a study of national importance.

"The nation in arms" is a term the meaning of which, before 1914, we had but vaguely conceived; we know now that it comprises much more than the men who bear arms. No democracy will consent to hand over to professional sailors, soldiers, and airmen the direction of the whole vast forces which comprise the power of a nation, as Ludendorff has more than once hinted, in his two books, that Germany should have done in the Great War. The instinct which forbids this is wise, for I do not believe that even Napoleon at his zenith could himself have controlled and directed the complex resources of a modern great Power and at the same time have commanded its armies in the field.

It is, then, agreed that the conduct of war must be directed by statesmen, and it is equally agreed that one part of the conduct of war, the handling of armies and navies, must be left to professional experts. How are these two conditions to be fulfilled?

In time of peace statesmen have at their elbow experts to assist them in the work of the departments with which they are charged. It is the statesman's business to inform his experts of the policy to which his Government is committed, and to explain to them his plans for giving effect to that policy. They have then to complete the details of such plans, to point out to the statesman difficulties in the way, and to suggest the best method of overcoming them. When, as sometimes happens, the statesman has no policy, it is the business of the expert to propose to him measures which his experience has told him are required. The statesman's function is then to tell his adviser how far the public is prepared to accept such measures; whether the political situation is ripe for their introduction. Under such conditions the expert is the servant of the statesman and through him of the State. He is usually anonymous and is unknown to the general public. A Chancellor of the Exchequer is not expected to be an expert financier and economist any more than a civilian statesman is expected to be an expert strategist and tactician. He gets such advice and help as he thinks necessary from financiers and economists, and accepts or rejects as much of that advice as he thinks fit. He makes himself responsible for the final result, which he himself presents through Parliament to the nation.

Why are not similar methods possible in war? If the statesman is primarily responsible for the conduct of war, why should he not explain his policy and his plans to his soldiers and sailors and get them to prepare the details for him, modify those details himself as seems to him fit, and supervise the execution of the plan as finally prepared?

The reason why this method is not applicable to the conduct of war is that war is neither a science nor a business; it is an art. The economist or the financier can say to his Chancellor, "Do this, and such and such will be the consequences. You will gain or lose so much revenue." The Chancellor can check that opinion with a dozen others, and, if he is a judge of men, he knows what value to place on each. Neither soldiers nor sailors, if they know their business, will attempt to prophesy how they will act before they meet their enemy, nor will they foretell what the results will be. They know that in war there are few constants and an immense number of variants. Like the painter or the sculptor, they should be guided automatically by the principles of their art, and should be so steeped in its technique that instinctively and without any conscious process of reasoning they apply the right stroke at the right time.

Foch is fond of quoting the question which General Verdy du Vernois asked himself when, in the Austro-Prussian War of 1866, he approached the battlefield of Nachod. ""Let history and principles go to the devil. After all, what is the problem?"[2] Which means that it is only the amateur who thinks of principles and technique when it is time to act, only the duffer at golf who murmurs to himself, "Slow back." If I want my portrait painted I select an artist whose terms are within my means and tell him the kind of portrait I want to have, but I do not expect him to be able to tell me beforehand how he is going to make me look, still less to explain to me the strokes by which he is going to produce his picture. If I don't like the portrait I can go to another artist, but it would not occur to me to tell the first how the portrait should have been painted.

Here, then, is one vitally important difference between the military experts and those other experts with whom statesmen are normally in contact. But there are others. The soldier or the sailor in command in war is never anonymous. He is a public figure, and the public regards him as directly responsible to it for the employment of the forces committed to his charge — forces in which serve the sons, brothers, sweethearts, and husbands of the nation. The statesman is apt to stress his responsibilities in time of war, and they are heavy, but those of the soldier and sailor are not less heavy. "Great results in war," says Foch, "are due to the commander. History is therefore right in making generals responsible for victories, in which case they are glorified, and for defeats, in which case they are disgraced."[3] The expert in the Government office does not win much glory, but he has little risk of disgrace.

The kind of expert the statesman has to use for the direction of armed forces in time of war is, then, very different from the kind of expert whom he uses in time of peace. The advice of the expert soldier and sailor cannot be treated like the advice of the expert financier, because it involves action which they alone can take. The statesman can present his budget, and he will rightly receive all the credit or blame for proposals which others may have prepared for him, because the responsibility for action is his; but he cannot lead armies and fleets against the foe, or be held responsible for the maneuvers of admirals and generals, though he may be called to account for his choice of commanders.

The military chief is, therefore, or should be, in a different relation to the statesman in time of war from that occupied by any of his assistants in time of peace. I have suggested that this relation should be of the nature of a partnership in which the statesman becomes the senior partner. If that is so, then it is clearly necessary that the conditions of the partnership and the functions of the partners should be determined beforehand. This is the more necessary because, just as the process of mobilization places armies and fleets on a footing very different from that which obtains in peace, so war places Government in a new position. But the process of mobilization is well known and its effect is studied beforehand — it is even occasionally practised in time of peace; but we have never, before we went into a war, considered what should be the machinery for its conduct, and those who had to use that machinery have never had an opportunity of examining the mechanism and of considering how it would work.

It is the practice in Great Britain and also in the United States — less invariably in other countries with a democratic system of government — to place civilian ministers in charge of the military departments. These ministers are responsible to Parliament — and through it to the country — for the whole of the administration of the services which they direct. Few would, I think, dispute that the definite assertion of civilian control over military force is necessary and desirable. As regards our army, that control has been established only after a protracted struggle between Crown and Parliament, which ended more recently than most people might imagine. It became finally effective in 1895, when the Duke of Cambridge resigned his position as Commander-in-Chief.

Speaking from his place in the House of Commons, Mr. (now Lord) Balfour said: "If the

Secretary of State is to take official advice from the Commander-in-Chief alone, it is absolutely impossible that he should be really responsible; in this House he will be no more than the mouthpiece of the Commander-in-Chief." I have always suspected that it was largely for the purpose of removing the last possibility of this danger that Mr. Balfour, when he became Prime Minister, abolished the office of Commander-in-Chief and created an Army Council. Be that as it may, we have in peace time a civilian minister in complete control of the army, while Mr. Churchill has reminded us in The World Crisis that when he entered the Admiralty he found himself "responsible to Crown and Parliament for all its business."[4]

I much doubt if Lord Balfour or any other stickler for the control of Parliament ever seriously intended that civilian ministers should prepare plans of campaign or direct the disposition of armies and navies in war. I am convinced that the great mass of voters took it for granted that such matters would be in the hands of military experts. Some reconsideration of the powers and functions of ministers when armies and navies are mobilized, some definite system for the conduct of war, should then have been prepared before war came upon us. As this was not done, we find that naturally enough the ministers in control of the naval and military departments continued in the early part of the Great War to exercise the powers conferred on them for the purpose of administration in time of peace. Mr. Churchill tells us, for instance, that toward the end of July, when the crisis appeared to be imminent, he prepared a list of seventeen points to be attended to, an early presage of the part points were to play in the war and its settlement.[5] These points included the dispositions of fleets from home waters to China. This was in no sense his business. All that it should have been necessary for him to do —and that he should have done when he entered the Admiralty in 1911, not when the crisis came — was to ask his naval advisers for their scheme of mobilization, and satisfy himself that it was complete. Mr. Churchill's points, of which he gives us a facsimile, are evidence of his prescience and foresight, but the matters with which they deal are not such as should be left to the prescience and foresight of any individual, and least of all to the chance of having an energetic and forceful minister in office when war is imminent. I do not suggest that they were so left, but I do suggest that the fact that Mr. Churchill prepared this list and has proudly exhibited it to us is evidence of an absence of system and a confusion of functions, which had, before long, disastrous consequences.

When the preparations for the Dardanelles expedition were under discussion we find that Mr. Churchill's naval advisers, grown accustomed to his domination, were in some uncertainty as to their powers and duties. They appear to have acquiesced in Lord Balfour's opinion — which, I have suggested, had only to do with administration in peace time —that the civilian minister was not to be the mere mouthpiece of his experts, but was to express and be responsible for his own opinions, and also to have accepted Mr. Churchill's view that he was "responsible to Crown and Parliament for all the business of the Admiralty." They did not conceive it to be their business to inform the War Council of the Cabinet where and why they differed from their civilian chief. The Royal Commission appointed to inquire-into the Dardanelles campaign says regarding this: —

If Lord Balfour is right as to the functions of

> We also think that the naval advisers should
> have expressed their views to the Council,
> whether asked or not, if they considered that
> the project which the Council was about to
> adopt was impracticable from a naval point
> of view. . . . We are unable to concur in the
> view put forward by Lord Fisher that it was
> his duty, if he differed from the chief of his
> department, to keep silence at the Council
> or to resign. We think that the adoption of
> any such principle generally would impair the
> efficiency of the public service.[6]

ministers in time of peace and the Royal Commissioners are right as to the functions of military
experts in time of war, there is evidently a marked
difference in the functions and duties of ministers
and military experts in peace and in war. In peace
the soldiers and sailors have to accept the policy
and the means provided for them by their political
chiefs, or resign. In war they become the advisers,
not of their ministers, but of the supreme authority in the State, and the ministers must therefore
automatically cease to be responsible for all the

business of their departments. There would therefore appear to be as much need for mobilizing a
system of government on the eve of war as for
mobilizing armies and fleets.

That this is so becomes even more evident
when we come to the administration of the War
Office in the early days of the war. A great military administrator was appointed War Secretary,
to the delight of the *Daily Mail,* which congrat-
ulated itself on appointing a man against whom
it was previously leading a campaign of attack.
When Lord Kitchener came into the War Office
he was lacking in experience in the methods of the
administration. 'of government at home, as was
Abraham Lincoln when he became President of
the United States. His work had lain entirely outside Great Britain. He found no suggestions for a
system of conducting war prepared for him and,
being at once involved in the huge task of raising
and equipping large armies, he had no time to give
consideration to that vital matter. It is not true to
say, as is sometimes said, that on the outbreak of
war the General Staff at the War Office scrambled
for places on the Headquarters Staff in France. I
was not on either myself at the time, so I can speak

freely. A definite plan for the mobilization of a headquarters in the field had been prepared as part of the systematic scheme of mobilization, and most of the appointments to that headquarters were provisionally made before the crisis came. But it is true that, in preparing the otherwise admirable scheme for placing our little army on a war footing, no thought had been given to the application of a similar measure either to the War Office in particular or to the Government as a whole.

Lord Kitchener, being a man of very strong character with a taste for centralization, in the absence of a considered system became not only Secretary of State for War, but also the chief military adviser of the Government, and to a great extent his own Chief of the Staff. It is in most circumstances beyond human capacity to combine the functions of three offices, and Lord Kitchener, who alone had seen from the first the magnitude of the task which we had undertaken and was endeavoring to provide us with armies adequate for that task, could not possibly perform them in the circumstances of the autumn of 1914. But his military advisers were no more clear than were Mr. Churchill's naval advisers as to their powers and duties, and in fact Lord Kitchener did act as their mouthpiece to the Government. The consequences of this state of affairs both in the naval and military departments is described by the Royal Commission in their investigation of the genesis of the Dardanelles campaign: —

Vagueness and want of precision are the inevitable consequence of absence of system and of a clear understanding by all concerned in the conduct of war, statesmen, soldiers, and sailors — of their functions and powers. These functions and powers can be exercised effectively only when those called upon to wield them know what they are and have had opportunity of studying them at first hand.

In what I have here said I do not wish to appear to be critical either of Lord Kitchener or of Mr. Churchill. We owe a debt of gratitude we can never repay to Lord Kitchener for foreseeing at once the length of the war, for taking the measure of the effort which we should be required to make, and for having faith in our power to create during the war a great national army —a faith which was shared by very few soldiers in 1914; to Mr. Churchill for the timely mobilization of our fleet

Mr. Churchill appears to have advocated the attack by ships alone before the War Council on a certain half-hearted and hesitating expert opinion, which favored a tentative or progressive scheme beginning with an attack on the outer forts. . . . There does not seem to have been direct support or direct opposition from the responsible naval and military advisers, Lord Fisher and Sir James Wolfe Murray, as to the practicability of carrying on the operations approved by the War Council, viz., to bombard and take the Gallipoli Peninsula with Constantinople as its objective. . . . It is impossible to read all the evidence, or to study the voluminous papers which have been submitted to us, without being struck with the atmosphere of vagueness and want of precision which seems to have characterized the proceedings of the War Council.[7]

and its dispatch to its war stations. We shall be hunting the wrong fox if we seek to attach to individuals the responsibilities which must be shared by statesmen, soldiers, and sailors, and indeed by all who have it in their power to form and guide public opinion. Having no system for the conduct of war, we were fortunate in having men of character and energy in the War Office and Admiralty.

(B) The System Needed

It was not until December 1915 that a definite system for the conduct of war was established in the War Office. It was created by Sir William Robertson, who, when he was offered the post of Chief of the Imperial General Staff at home, wrote to Lord Kitchener: — [8]

Then follow proposals for placing the organization of the War Office on a war footing.

There is in this document no suggestion of military domination. The War Council, which was to be "in the position of the commander of the whole of the Imperial Land Forces,'" was comprised exclusively of civilian ministers. What Sir William Robertson's proposals did do was to define clearly the respective functions of ministers and soldiers in war, — to set forth the terms of the partnership, — and they made a drastic change in the peace-time functions of the ministers who had charge of the army and navy. They were no longer

1. There should be a supreme directing authority whose function is to formulate policy, to decide on the theatres in which military operations are to be conducted, and to determine the relative importance of those theatres. This authority must also exercise a general supervision over the conduct of the war, and must select the men who are to execute the policy on which it has decided. Its constitution must be such that it is able to come to quick decisions, and therefore as regards the conduct of the war it must be absolute. The War Council should be capable of performing the functions of this supreme authority, provided it is relieved of responsibility to the Cabinet as a whole as regards the conduct of military operations, and that it has real executive power and is not merely an advisory committee.

The War Council will frequently find itself in a position similar to that of a commander in the field — that is, it will have to come to a decision when the situation is obscure, when information is deficient, and when the wishes and the powers of our Allies are uncertain. Whatever those difficulties may be, if and when a decision is required, it must be made. If it is deferred success cannot be expected, the commander concerned will have a grossly unfair burden placed upon him — in fact the absence of a decision may be little less than criminal, because of the loss of life which may be entailed.

2. In order that the War Council may be able to come to timely decisions on the questions with which it has to deal, it is essential that it should receive all advice on matters concerning military operations through one authoritative channel only. With us that channel must be the Chief of the Imperial General Staff. It is his function, as far as regards military operations, to present to the War Council his reasoned opinion as to che military effects of the policy which they propose, and as to the means of putting that approved policy into execution. The War

Council is therefore to accept or reject the reasoned advice so offered.

Advice regarding military operations emanating from members of the Cabinet or of the War Council in their individual capacity, or from any other individual, should be sifted, examined, and presented, if necessary, with reasoned conclusions, to the War Council by the Chief of the Imperial General Staff before it is accepted by the War Council.

3. All military operations required to put into execution the policy approved by the War Council should be issued and signed by the Chief of the Imperial General Staff, under the authority of the Secretary of State for War, mot under that of the War Council. Similarly all communications from general officers commanding regarding military operations should be addressed to the Chief of the Imperial General Staff. In fact the same procedure is required in London as obtains in the field, the War Council being in the position of the commander of the whole of the Imperial

> Land Forces and, with the War _ Office Staff,
> constituting the Great General Headquarters
> of the Empire.

entirely responsible to Crown and Parliament for all the business of their departments.

The effect of these proposals was to bring about an immediate improvement in the business of conducting the war. One gentleman who had been during a long life in intimate touch with the management of public affairs told me a short time after the new system had been at work that he never remembered so remarkable a change from scurry and confusion to order and method. Such difficulties as subsequently arose were in part due . to a Clash of personalities — which no system can prevent — and in part due to unwillingness on the part of certain ministers to apply a system with which they were unfamiliar, and which they did not entirely understand. That difficulty is avoidable if the system is prepared and known beforehand. When Mr. Lloyd George became Prime Minister in December 1916, he improved the organization for the conduct of the war

by abolishing the existing Cabinet with its War
Council or Committee and substituting a small
War Cabinet of five ministers.[9] "'From a military
standpoint,'" says Sir William Robertson, who had
longer experience of the War Cabinet than any
other soldier or sailor, "and leaving out of account
the constitutional aspect of the question, — about
which I express no opinion, — the change was
welcome, if only for the reason that six men could
be trusted to give a decision in less time than a
score would, but my experience leads me to add
that the War Cabinet did not by any means provide a complete remedy for the evils from which
its predecessor had suffered. Most of its members
were ministers without portfolios, and, having
little if any firsthand knowledge of the questions
with which they had to deal, were necessarily
dependent upon those ministers who had it. Consequently the Secretary of State for War, the First
Lord of the Admiralty, and the Foreign Secretary,
none of whom was a member of the War Cabinet,
usually had to attend once a day when meetings
were held, while other ministers, such as the Secretary of State for India, the Shipping Controller,
the Minister of Labor, the Minister of Air, and the

Minister of Munitions had also frequently to be summoned. The result was that the total number present was often not much less than, and was sometimes more than, under the old system, and it is difficult to see how this could have been prevented; for, whether the heads of the various state departments do or do not permanently belong to the body charged with the supreme direction of a war, they must be called in when important questions concerning their departments are being considered. The fact is that in a great war such as that of 1914-18 the ramifications of the numerous problems which arise are so widespread that the rapid dispatch of business must always be exceedingly difficult to achieve."[10]

There was a further difficulty which Sir William Robertson does not mention. The War Cabinet naturally required the daily attendance at its meetings of its chief military and naval advisers. This took up a very great deal of valuable time, and usually kept these high functionaries from their offices for the greater part of the morning.

Now Sir William Robertson's system, established after fifteen months of the war, at a time when grievous experience showed that there was something vitally wrong with our methods of conducting war, was — save in one respect — very similar to that established by Abraham Lincoln in March 1864. Then Halleck became Lincoln's Chief of the Staff, and communicated the views of the administration in Washington to Grant, the commander in the field, and with Halleck Grant, save very exceptionally, corresponded. The one important difference was that Lincoln was his own War Cabinet. The Constitution of the United States permits this. Is there anything in our Constitution which prevents us from adopting a similar procedure? We have seen that the experience of war caused us to modify very materially the constitutional powers of the Secretary of State for War, and of the First Lord of the Admiralty, as they existed in peace and were used in the early days of the struggle. We have seen that Mr. Lloyd George formed a Cabinet of a kind strange to our constitutional practice. What is there to prevent. us from going a step further?

The practice of Rome and of the United States should assure us that there is nothing undemocratic in establishing a temporary dictatorship in time of national emergency. We must, in a great war, have a supreme authority to direct all the armed forces of the Empire. That authority must be civil, and it is far better that it should be vested in a man than in a committee. That man with us must be the Prime Minister. I suggest that we should be well advised, whenever such a danger arises as calls for the mobilization of the whole of our forces, to place in the hands of the Prime Minister authority to nominate and remove his military advisers and the commanders of armies and fleets, and to conduct in consultation with these advisers the naval, military, and air operations of the war. The Order in Council, or other instrument which confers this power on the Prime Minister, should at the same time define exactly the powers and functions and responsibilities of his military advisers. The initial policy of the Government in the war, relations with friendly or neutral States, the raising and distribution of man power, the conservation and development of the resources of the State and the means of adding to them, the regulation of home affairs — all these are matters which can well be discussed in Cabinet or committee, but the whole history of war shows us plainly that a committee is not a suitable body to direct military operations.

It is more than two hundred years since the Duke of Marlborough expressed his opinion of War Cabinets. On August 2, 1705, he wrote to the Pensioner of Holland: —

We may consider ourselves to be reasonably secure against private animosities of the kind that vexed Marlborough, but "the secrecy and dispatch upon which all great undertakings depend" are more likely to be obtained if the military advisers have to deal with one man instead of a committee. It is also far more likely that relations of intimacy and mutual confidence — which, as I have endeavored to show, are one of the essential factors of success — will be more successfully established if the military advisers are brought into direct contact with the Prime Minister than if they have to deal with a Cabinet, limited though it be in numbers.

There are few questions more difficult for those charged with the direction of armies and navies than that upon which Marlborough touches in the second paragraph of his letter: How much and how little of military plans should be disclosed

I am very uneasy in my own mind to see how everything here is like to go notwithstanding the superiority and the goodness of our troops, which ought to make us not doubt of success. However, it is certain that, if affairs continue in the same policy they now are, it will be impossible to attempt anything considerable with advantage, since councils of war must be called upon every occasion, which entirely destroys the secrecy and dispatch upon which all great undertakings depend, and has unavoidably another very unhappy effect, for, the private animosities between so many persons as have to be assembled being so great, and their inclinations and interests so different as always to make one party oppose what the other advises, they consequently never agree.

I do not say this because I have the honor of being at the head of the army, but it is absolutely necessary that such power be lodged with the general as may enable him to act as he thinks proper, according to the best of his judgment, without being obliged ever to communicate what he intends further than he thinks convenient.

to ministers? There are certain matters, as I have pointed out, upon which they have an undeniable right to information. They must be assured that the plans proposed are within the means of the nation; they must equally be assured that the vitals of the nation are to be sufficiently protected. They are entitled to receive every scrap of information about operations which are completed, that they may be able to judge of the capacity of their commanders, but the minister who seeks information beforehand as to when and how a battle will be fought, and what its result will be, is ignorant of his business. He should recall Lincoln's interview with Grant. A committee is usually more inquisitive than an individual, and if the military advisers have to do with one minister instead of with half a dozen it will be the easier to hold the balance between the advantages of secrecy and the disadvantages of failing to satisfy that minister's legitimate anxieties.

On all these grounds, then, I believe that the supreme directing authority over all the forces of the Empire in time of war should be one man, and that man the Prime Minister, just as in the United States of America the supreme authority is the President. We have of recent years taken one very satisfactory measure for the establishment of such a system of conducting war. In 1923 the Prime Minister appointed a committee to inquire into national and imperial defense. This committee recommended, among other measures, that: "In addition to the functions of the Chiefs of the Staff[11] as advisers on questions of sea, land, or air policy, respectively, to their own Board or Council, each of the three Chiefs of the Staff will have an individual and collective responsibility for advising on defense policy as a whole, the three constituting as it were a super-chief of a War Staff in Commission. In carrying out this function they will meet together for the discussion of questions which affect their joint |responsibilities."[12] This is a great step forward in the coordination of the three services. Let us complete it by arranging for the ~ coordination of policy and strategy. "A Super-Chief of a War Staff in Commission" connotes yet another chief whom these three are to serve. Let that chief be created and let his functions be defined. If the conferring of so much power on one man be too much for our Constitutionalists to swallow, then let there be a War Cabinet as small as possible, and, just as soldiers and sailors know what their positions and functions will be on mobilization and are prepared to step into them at a moment's notice, let ministers also know theirs. There will then be some prospect that they will study their duties and be ready to learn something of what the history of war has to teach.

(C) Statesmen, Soldiers, and People

*Fools," wrote Bismarck, "say they learn from their own experience. I have always contrived to get my experience at the expense of others." We might have learned from the experience of Germany how to create a system for the conduct of war. We did not do so, because we did not fully understand what that experience was. We were disposed to think that Germany's striking military success in 1866 and 1870 was due entirely to her methods of training soldiers and the organization of her General Staff. When towards the end of his life von Moltke said that in whatever direction other nations might develop their strength Germany would remain superior in the command, most of us thought that he was referring to the German General Staff system. We were, I think, wrong in this. Von Moltke meant that Germany had thought out a system for the conduct of war and the other nations had not. When mobilization was ordered, the old King William, Bismarck, and von Roon knew their duties and places as thoroughly as did the humblest reservist tramping to his place of muster. This was not because they wore the *pickelhaube*[13] instead of the top hat, but because they had thought about the matter. We know now that there was a defect in von Moltke's system. It did not provide for the fact which von Moltke had not foreseen, that in the modern nation in arms the military part in the combined effort is but twenty-five per cent of the whole. So, when the system was directed by second-rate men in 1914, the immediate military advantage to be gained by violating the frontier of Belgium was seized and the consequences of tearing up a treaty in the eyes of the world were overlooked. There was at no time much fear that we should give the military element in any system for the conduct of the war excessive prominence, and we might, had we been ready to learn from the experiences of others, have taken the good in von Moltke's plans and adapted them to our use. That good was the outcome neither of militarism nor of Prussianism, but of thought and common sense.

Were we shy of turning to Prussia for lessons in political science, we might have learned from the experience of Abraham Lincoln, who when he visited the armies of the Union did wear a top hat. We had gone into the war against. Russia in 1854 with a system which invited defeat. 'The expedient," says Kinglake, "of dividing the control of our army between the Sovereign and the Sovereign's Government continued to work its effects upon our military administration throughout the time of the Regency, throughout the two reigns that followed; and even after that time, during many a year, there was no removal of the constitutional deformity, no abatement of the evil it caused.

"A due sense of justice, however, commands us to remember and own that, before our quarrel with Russia and indeed until several years afterwards, the idea of constituting a War Department upon sound principles had not passed through that long ordeal of discussion which is commonly required in England for the ripening of great public questions."[14]

The long ordeal of discussion lasted more than fifty years. It left us eventually with a reorganized War Department and General Staff, but we had not in August 1914 reached the position at which Lincoln had arrived in March 1864. We had not got so far even as considering the organization of the great General Headquarters of the Empire, the establishment of a system for the conduct of war.

One of the reasons why we did not learn what to my thinking is the chief lesson of the American Civil War is that this subject has been curiously neglected by British students of war.[15] Hamley does not mention it. Henderson, who more than any other has moulded modern British military opinion, in his life of Stonewall Jackson was concerned with the least fortunate period of Lincoln's war administration. He devoted a good many pages to the evils of civilian control and makes but a brief reference to Lincoln's abdication of his military functions in Grant's favor. The consequence of this is that it has been a common practice for

British writers on military matters to fulminate against political interference in strategy, and it has not been difficult for them to find numerous instances both in the history of the American Civil War and in that of other wars in which political interference has been utterly mischievous. These fulminations leave the statesman cold, because he is aware that there must be civilian control of strategy, and he is therefore apt to ascribe them either to military ignorance of political science or to the soldiers' lust of power.

I think it is true to say that the general impression in the minds of students of the American Civil War is that Lincoln, great as he was, failed as a wat minister save when he handed over the entire direction of military affairs to Grant. I have endeavored to show that this is not a correct judgment. The fathers of the study of strategy, Jomini and Clausewitz, both recognized that political control is not merely unavoidable but essential. Clausewitz, who wrote the military gospel of the most militaristic of modern Powers, said: "None of the main plans which are necessary for a war can be made without insight into the political relations, and people say something quite different from what they mean when they talk of the harmful influence of policy on the conduct of war. It is not the influence but the policy they should blame. If the policy is sound, — that is, if it hits the mark, — it can affect the war only in its own sense and only advantageously; and when this influence diverts the war from its purpose the source must be sought in a mistaken policy."[16] We may, I think, carry Clausewitz's conclusion a stage further, and say from the experiences of the American Civil War, and of the Great War, that it is necessary that both policy and strategy should be sound, and that statesman and soldier should mutually understand each other's functions and needs. Jefferson Davis had no clear policy, and a brilliant soldier could not win victory without that aid which policy should have given. The Confederate President cannot, as I have tried to show, fairly be charged with undue interference with the operations of his generals in the field; the charge rather should be that he did not interfere enough and in the right way. Abraham Lincoln had a very definite and entirely sound policy from the beginning of the war, but he did not know how to translate that policy into instructions to McClellan, and McClellan did not know what advice to give his political chief, nor indeed was he aware that it was his duty to advise him at all.

The Clausewitzian method of the abstract study of these problems is not one which is calculated to rouse much interest save in a few professional students, and that does not suffice. If we are to deal effectively with that great evil, war, when it comes, then the methods of dealing with it must be understood by all men and women of intelligence who have the interests of their country at heart. If we leave the organization of government in time of war to be evolved by experience, then, history tells us, we shall have to buy that experience at a terrible price.

I do not believe that we are at all likely to be involved in another great war for many years to come. There are, in Europe especially, millions of men and women who have had the bitterest experiences of war, and I can hardly conceive it to be possible that while the majority of these are alive they will permit Europe to become involved in another cataclysm. I believe also that the majority of the statesmen of Europe are conscious that if another great war comes before the wounds of the last are fully healed it will bring with it utter ruin and desolation. I have great hopes that the authority and influence of the League of Nations will eventually be such as to make war on a great scale impossible. But no one can say that this is so yet. Even the Covenant of the League envisages the possibility of war, and while war is a possibility it behooves the many among us who have had experience of war to ponder these things, and to leave to our descendants a better system of conducting war than we enjoyed.

It is in the hope that some who would not read an abstract and technical study may take an interest in the experience of men who figure largely in the pages of history, that I have adopted a different method from that of Clausewitz.

But it may be said, if a great war is not likely to break out again for many years, why all this pother? Such a war will most certainly be as different in character from the last war as that was different from the American Civil War. How can we devise now a system which will meet unknown requirements? It may be that in the next war machines will be many and men few; that it will no longer be a question of employment of millions in the field, but of employing those millions in workshops and factories.

I am not going to be so foolish as to prophesy what form war will take ten, twenty, or fifty years hence, but human experience shows that when a system exists it is no hard matter to modify it to meet changing conditions, and that when no system exists the creation of one in emergency is both difficult and costly. That is why we should, while experience is fresh in our minds, devote some thought to that experience.

It seems far from certain that we have even yet got our minds clear on the question of the relations between statesmen and soldiers in war. Mr. Churchill has published a brilliant defense of his conduct in the Admiralty, from which it would appear to be still his firm belief that it is a part of the business of civilian ministers to prepare plans of campaign. Sir William Robertson says: —

Since the war I have heard more than one minister express views similar to those of Sir William Robertson's interlocutor, and indeed I have very little doubt that most ministers and ex-ministers alive to-day are of the same mind.

Who is right, the statesman or the soldier?

> A minister once tried in the course of conversation to persuade me that the duty of a professional adviser begins and ends with giving his advice, and that after it has been given and ministers have considered it, the orders of the Government should be carried out without further question or remonstrance. I was unable to agree with him as to the chief professional adviser, holding that he had a duty to the country as well as to the ministers, and I said so, though I admitted that only special circumstances would justify the conclusion that duty to ministers conflicted with duty to country, and must accordingly take second place.[17]

This is a matter on which there should be no possibility of doubt. There can be no effective codperation between ministers and soldiers while doubt remains. I have already described the essential difference between the military and the civilian expert adviser of a Government, but I must for a moment return to this point. The civil servant can be trusted to carry out the plans of the

Government, even when he does not agree with them, and after he has expressed that disagreement to his political chief. But a soldier in war cannot do the same, because in war the moral element is predominant. It is not in human nature for a man to prosecute wholeheartedly a plan which involves great risks and the lives of others, if he does not believe in it absolutely. Further, just as a good horse knows at once when his rider is funking[18] the hedge ahead and refuses when he comes to it, so an army is instantly conscious of any lack of faith, any weakening of purpose, in its leaders. The soldier who attempts to carry out a plan with which he disagrees is therefore failing in duty to his country.

If these things are not known, it can only be because they are not studied, not because of any lack of evidence of their truth.

There is another reason for seeking to create some greater interest than is at present taken in this all-important matter of relations between soldiers and statesmen. Public opinion has become an element of the first importance in the conduct of war. I am among those who believe that in future wars the prime object of the contending nations will not be the destruction of the opposing forces, but what the Germans call the will to victory of the opposing peoples. The immense extent of the increase of the zone of danger, due to the introduction of aircraft, has, it is generally admitted, brought the civil population into a jeopardy almost if not quite as great as that which confronts those who bear arms. The morale of the nation is therefore likely to be as important a factor in war as the morale of armies has always been. The defeat of the enemy's main forces, hitherto held to be the first aim of strategy, becomes only means to an end, which may be obtained even without those means. For a people may find the continuance of war to be intolerable. The statesman who can hold a nation to its purpose, as Lincoln did in July and August 1864, is to-day as necessary as was and is the general who can rally the drooping energies and spirits of a weary army for a further effort. In a long and fiercely contested war there comes a time when exhausted human nature craves for any alternative to conditions which seem beyond endurance. Then the most gallant spirits lose confidence, the less brave become craven, and it is then that "the spark in the breast of the commander must rekindle hope in the hearts of his men, and so long as he is equal to his task he remains their commander. When his influence ceases and his own spirit is no longer strong enough to revive the spirit of others, the masses, drawing him with them, sink into the lower region of animal nature which recoils from danger and knows not shame. Such are the obstacles which the brain and courage of the military commander must overcome if he is to make his name illustrious."[19]

The qualities which Clausewitz required of his general at the beginning of the nineteenth century are to-day also required of the statesman-leader of the nation in arms. But if statesman and soldier are to accomplish their hard tasks they must be protected against the pressure and abuse of the ignorant. The mischief which an ill-informed public opinion could do in wars of the past, in which it was subjected to no such strain as it may have to endure in wars of the future, is clear to anyone who cares to read the history of war. Clamor in the press for the removal of this statesman or that soldier may, if it is made without knowledge of what the conduct of war is and requires, cause the downfall of a Lincoln, a Lee, or a Grant.

As long as war is a possibility, we need as a beginning of preparation that there be a system of government in time of war known and understood by statesmen, soldiers, and people, or at least by those who guide public opinion, and that the precise functions of ministers and military chiefs in that system be clearly defined. One of the reasons why almost every war upon which we have entered for the last hundred and fifty years has begun disastrously for us is that we have never understood the difference between government in peace and in war. We have tried slowly and painfully to adapt the peace machinery during the struggle to purposes for which it was never intended.

War may be likened to epidemic disease. The first object is to prevent the occurrence of the evil. That is the task of one kind of expert, who discovers the cause of the disease, isolates the germ, and prepares the antitoxin. If the evil comes, specialist and medical practitioner work together, each in his own rôle, to drive off the disease with the least possible loss of life, but the task of both is rendered tenfold more difficult if they are dealing with an ignorant people who know not the virtues of cleanliness and sanitation, who mistrust and resist their efforts to heal. So it is with war. The first task of the statesman is to prevent it by discovering and removing its causes. In that task he needs the intelligent cooperation of the people. If war comes, he calls in the soldier practitioner, but again the cooperation of the people is required. The three, statesman, soldier, and people, can work together in harmony only when the duties and functions of each are understood by all.

Notes:

1. Robertson: *From Private to Field Marshal,* p. 322.

2. Foch: *The Principles of War,* p. 14.

3. *Ibid.,* p. 288. Foch is here speaking of operations in the field — not of the conduct of war.

4. Churchill: *The World Crisis, 1911-14,* p. 70.

5. *Ibid,* p. 194.

6. Royal Commission, *Dardanelles Expedition,* N. 43. One of the Commissioners, the Rt. Hon. Andrew Fisher, disagreed with his colleagues and said, "I dissent in the strongest terms from any suggestion that the departmental advisers of a

minister in his company at a council meeting should express any
views at all other than to the minister and through him, unless specifically invited to do so" (*Report*, p. 44).

7. Royal Commission, Dardanelles Expedition, N. 43, *Report,* pp. 41 and 21.

8. Robertson: *From Private to Field Marshal,* p. 239.

9. A sixth — General Smuts — was subsequently added.

10. Robertson: *From Private to Field Marshal,* p. 253.

11. Of Army, Navy, and Air Force.

12. Report of the Sub-Committee of the Committee of Imperial Defense, 1924, Cmd. 3029, para. 51 CL).

13. Editor's note: The *pickelhaube* is the spiked, Prussian helmet.

14. Kinglake: *The Invasion of the Crimea,* vol. VII, p. 81.

15. Amongst the few exceptions are Mr. Spenser Wilkinson and General Sir G. Aston.

16. Clausewitz: *Vom Kriege,* Book VIII.

17. Robertson: *From Private to Field Marshal,* p. 255.

18. Editor's note: *Funking:* the present participle of *to funk,* which is to avoid something out of fear. From the Flemish, *fonck*: avoidance or disturbance. *Archaic, particularly English.*

19. Clausewitz: *Vom Kriege,* Book VI.